REFERENCE

FOR REFERENCE

Do Not Take From This Room

INDIA

Radhika Srinivasan

MARSHALL CAVENDISH
New York • London • Sydney

Reference edition published 1992 by
Marshall Cavendish Corporation
2415 Jerusalem Avenue
North Bellmore
New York 11710

Editorial Director	Shirley Hew
Managing Editors	Mark Dartford
	Shova Loh
Editors	Goh Sui Noi
	Meena Mylvaganam
	Cheryl M. English
Picture Editor	Jane Duff
Production	Jeremy Chan
	Robert Paulley
	Julie Cairns
Design	Tuck Loong
	Doris Nga
	Stella Liu
	Lee Woon Hong
Illustrators	Francis Oak
	Thomas Koh
	Vincent Chew

Printed in Singapore

Library of Congress Cataloging-in-Publication Data:
Srinivasan, 1951–
     India / by Srinivasan—Reference ed.
      p. cm.—(Cultures Of The World)
     Includes bibliographical references.
     Summary: Introduces the geography,
history, religious beliefs, government, and people
of India.
     ISBN 1 85435 515 5
     1. India—Juvenile literature. [1. India.]
I. Title. II. Series.
DS407.S73 1990
954—dc20   89-25466
                          CIP
                          AC

INTRODUCTION

INDIA has an almost physical impact on its visitors, so vivid are the contrasts. The Indians, an estimated 835 million in 1988, are a larger variety of races than may be found in any other country in the world. There are seventeen official languages, and even these cannot be said to represent the entire population. There are Indians living in lavish bungalows and Indians living on city pavements, braving freezing winters and heat-wave summers. India's history, which goes back five thousand years, lives on in its literature, religions and architecture. Here, too, contrasts are vivid: diverse religions co-exist while splendid Mughal minarets and monumental Hindu gateways tower close to colonial Portuguese and British architecture.

In the pages of this book, India's rich and varied cultural heritage is described with the help of color illustrations. The book is one of a series, *Cultures of the World*—a look at people and their lifestyles around the world.

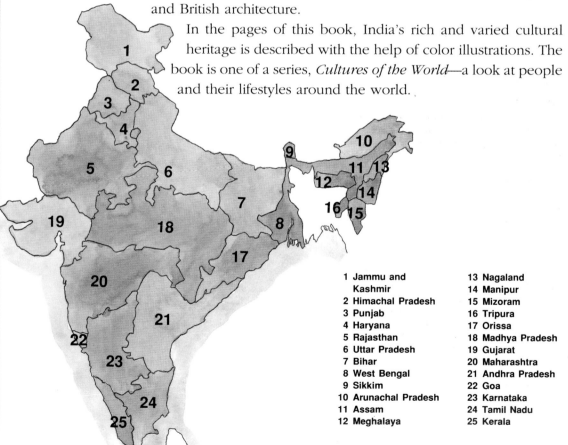

1 Jammu and Kashmir	13 Nagaland
2 Himachal Pradesh	14 Manipur
3 Punjab	15 Mizoram
4 Haryana	16 Tripura
5 Rajasthan	17 Orissa
6 Uttar Pradesh	18 Madhya Pradesh
7 Bihar	19 Gujarat
8 West Bengal	20 Maharashtra
9 Sikkim	21 Andhra Pradesh
10 Arunachal Pradesh	22 Goa
11 Assam	23 Karnataka
12 Meghalaya	24 Tamil Nadu
	25 Kerala

CONTENTS

Feeding the rats of Rajasthan.

CONTENTS

Family portrait. Earthy colors of house and urn set off the brilliant clothes and decor.

5

GEOGRAPHY

PHYSICAL FEATURES

INDIA IS about one-third the size of the United States of America. With an area of 1.27 million square miles, it is the seventh largest country in the world. It is a subcontinent, bounded by the Himalayas in the north and vast seas on the other three sides. In the east is the Bay of Bengal, and in the west, the Arabian Sea. Both stretch southward to join the Indian Ocean.

The Himalayan mountains extend over a distance of 1,490 miles from the northern state of Jammu to the eastern border state of Arunachal Pradesh. One of the largest mountain chains in the world, the Himalayas include the world's tallest peaks.

At either end of the Himalayas there are other mountain chains, with a few passes providing a respite. The Khyber and Bolan passes in the northwest are particularly significant because they were the entry points for several foreign invaders who marched upon India in the course of its eventful history.

Nepal and China are India's northern neighbors. Afghanistan and Pakistan are to its northwest, while Burma and Bangladesh are to its east. Sri Lanka lies to its south, barely an hour's boat-ride from the subcontinent's southern tip. In the southeast, very close to Indonesia, are India's Andaman and Nicobar islands.

Opposite: **India's roof—the Ladakh plateau of Kashmir.**

Below: **Children of India's warm central region.**

7

MOUNTAINS AND RIVERS

India can be divided roughly into three geographical regions: the mountainous Himalayan North, the Indo-Gangetic plain, and the Southern peninsula known as the Deccan.

The Himalayas provide the country with three major rivers—the Indus, the Ganges and the Brahmaputra. The Ganges, which Indians consider the holiest of the rivers, flows from the Himalayas all the way through Varanasi and Bengal, making fertile the entire region known as the Indo-Gangetic plain. Most of the Indus waters flow into Pakistan, and a large part of the Brahmaputra flows into Bangladesh.

While the rivers in the North are snow-fed, most of the rivers in the South are rain-fed and so fluctuate in volume. Godavari, Krishna, Mahanadi and Cauvery rivers make peninsular India fertile.

The Indo-Gangetic plain, because of the abundant water supply, has rich alluvial soil and is the most densely populated region of India. In contrast, the triangular region south of the plain is a rather rocky, uneven plateau. Bordering this plateau on either side are the smaller mountains known as the Eastern and Western Ghats.

Though the coastline is long, natural harbors are few and far between. The coastline has undergone changes in the past, leaving ancient ports such as Tamluk in the East, Kaveripatnam in the South and Lothal in the West landlocked today.

Opposite top: **Ladakh family of the Himalayas.**

Below: **Holy dip in a river.**

The Vindhya mountains and the Narmada river are located between the South and the North. As a result, the history of the two regions has often taken different courses.

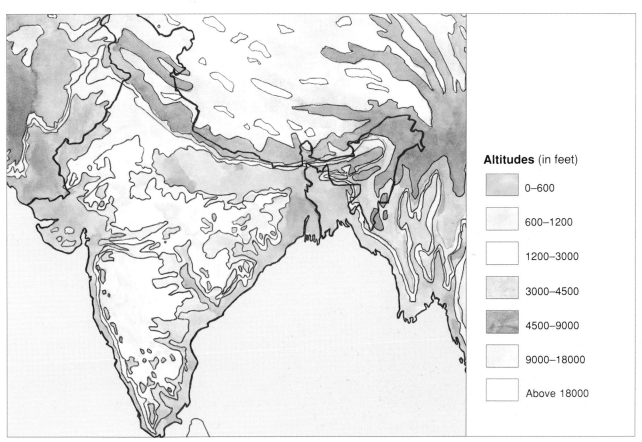

Altitudes (in feet)

0–600

600–1200

1200–3000

3000–4500

4500–9000

9000–18000

Above 18000

SEASONS AND CLIMATE

India's climate varies from torrid to arctic, depending on the region and the season. The fertile valleys of Kashmir and Simla in the North are delightfully cool in the summer months (April to June), but turn icy cold in December/January, reaching temperatures below freezing point. The central heartland, on the other hand, can broadly be described as tropical.

There are six seasons in India: winter, spring, summer, summer monsoon, autumn and winter monsoon. The climate is affected by two seasonal winds, the northeast monsoon wind and the southeast monsoon wind.

Rainfall also varies from region to region. In the East Indian state of Assam near the Khasi hills, the annual rainfall is as high as 430 inches. Chirapunji in the East has recorded the highest annual rainfall in the world (1,042 inches)!

In Bombay and the Western Ghats, June to September are wet months, with rainfall reaching 118 inches. While New Delhi experiences thunder showers preceded by dust storms in July/August, Madras and the South get most of their rain in December. In the hot season, the weather can be very oppressive, with temperature rising to 122°F in Central India.

Failure of the winds to produce sufficient rain occasionally causes drought and famine, while excessive rain now and then causes flash floods and severe loss of life. In an agricultural country such as India, the farmers are at the mercy of the rains. This explains why they often pray to the rain god, Varuna, either to protect them from floods or to bless them with abundant rain.

A field of wild mustard is a common sign of spring.

NATURAL RESOURCES

India's varied climate provides a rich vegetation. The Himalayan region is well-wooded with pines and conifers. The Eastern region has luxuriant forests and thick clumps of bamboo. India has 650 million hectares of forests and about 45,000 plant species, many of which are not found anywhere else in the world. To protect the land, there are protected reserves, but regrettably trees are still being cut down for fuel.

India has most of the mineral deposits it needs, including iron ore, coal, lignite, silver, copper, gold and zinc. Coal and lignite account for more than 60% of India's energy consumption. Together with wood, oil and natural gas, India is almost self-sufficient in its energy needs.

India is rich in valuable timber. Lumber firms operate outside protected reserves.

INDIA'S WILDLIFE

India, the land of tigers and snakes, is in fact home to more than 850 animal species and 2,000 bird species. Many of them are exclusive to the subcontinent. No less than 63 national parks and 350 sanctuaries protect these animals, which include many wildcats: the snow leopard and the spotted cheetah are unique to Indian forests.

Another Indian animal, better known for its domestication and the part it plays during temple and palace ceremonies, is the Indian elephant. So common are the wild "tuskers" in the Mudumalai sanctuary of the South and the Assam forests of the East, at times they stray into homes and destroy gardens! Poaching is banned, yet sadly many of these majestic creatures are still hunted for their tusks, which fetch a fabulous price.

The bison, buffalo, nilgai (cross between a giraffe and an antelope) and the black buck are some other common animals of India. One-horn rhinoceroses, jackals and monkeys of different kinds are also found in Central Indian jungles.

Birds that live in this subcontinent range from tiny sunbirds no bigger than butterflies to cranes and vultures. Wild peacocks, brilliantly colored pheasants and fowls abound in Rajasthan, where one can see migratory Siberian cranes flying south to nest in December/January.

POPULATION

India's population was estimated to be 835 million in 1988, although the official census (taken once in 10 years) in 1981 put the number at 685.2 million. India is the second most populated country in the world, and the population is growing by 2.2% each year. At this rate, it is expected to cross the one billion mark by the turn of the century. Overpopulation is India's biggest problem.

As India is an agricultural country, the majority (over 70%) are farmers. Many have had little or no formal education. Generally, they live in large joint families where five or six children per couple is quite common. Life in a village is just as it was in the distant past.

In sharp contrast are the cities which face great problems of urbanization. Current estimates put Bombay as the largest Indian city with a population of 16.2 million, nearly double its size in 1981. Madras, New Delhi, Calcutta and Bangalore are some of the other overpopulated cities. Each day about 2,000 people migrate from the villages to Bombay alone, in search of work.

Most urban homes are nuclear families with two or three children. While cities like Bombay and Calcutta have India's very rich class of movie stars and businessmen residing in luxurious bungalows, they also have thousands of very poor and ill-fed people living in shanty slums, on pavements or roadsides.

Opposite top: **Indian elephant.**

Opposite bottom: **One-horn rhinoceroses.**

Below: **Some of India's millions assembled at the India Gate grounds of New Delhi.**

HISTORY

INDUS TO INDIA

INDIA'S PAST is deeply linked with the river Indus, which flows for about 1,242 miles from the Himalayan mountains to the Arabian Sea. The Indians called the river Sindhu and the Persians referred to it as the Hindu. The Greeks called it the Indus and gave the land its present name.

India's history goes back more than five thousand years. In 1924, archeologists discovered two very ancient cities in what is Pakistan today, Mohenjo-Daro and Harappa. The Indian sites are Ropar in Punjab and Kalibangan in Rajasthan, along the Indus. Houses made of burned bricks, a well laid out drainage system and clay seals bearing a script were found in these sites, indicating a highly advanced Indus valley civilization dating from around 2500 B.C.

It is believed that the people of the Indus valley were Dravidian, the indigenous Indian race. Sometime around 1500 B.C., another race known as the Aryans (Indo-Europeans, possibly from Iran) seems to have advanced into India and mingled with the prevailing race. The Aryans brought another culture with them, the Vedic culture.

The word *Veda* means "knowledge" in Sanskrit. Hymns contained in the four *Books of Knowledge*, known as the *Vedas*, were composed in this period, the Vedic period. They are primarily verses concerning the origin of life and glorifying nature, personified in, for example, Agni the fire god and Varuna the rain god.

In the Later Vedic period, the forces of nature were personified into *Devas* or gods and worshiped with rituals, sacrifices and recitation of Vedic hymns. To this day, priests chant these hymns during Hindu ceremonies in homes and temples.

Opposite: **Bronze figurine of Lord Shiva, a Hindu god that takes many forms, from the Chola period (8th–11th centuries A.D.). Here he is the Lord of Dance (*Nataraja*), his movements symbolizing the cosmic forces of nature.**

Buddha means "the one who knows." Prince Sidhartha, as he was known, was born in the year 520 B.C. at Kapilavastu in Nepal. He lived in luxury, free of sorrow, married at sixteen and had a son, Rahul. One day, he set out from his palace and saw a feeble old man. Next day, he saw a sick man, and the very next day, a corpse being taken for cremation. It was Prince Sidhartha's first experience of illness and death.

Greatly pained and moved, he renounced everything and went in search of answers to the cause of human misery. After a period of meditation, he received a vision of enlightenment. Since then he has been known as the Buddha.

BIRTH OF RELIGIONS

Arya means "noble" and the Aryans believed they were nobler than the Dravidians who cultivated the land. The Aryans divided society into four social classes, based on occupation: Brahmins, the priestly class; Kshatriyas, the ruling class; Vaishyas, the merchant class; and Sudras, the laboring class. Gradually these class distinctions became rigid and hereditary, because work was always handed down from father to son.

The post-Vedic period saw the birth of many Sanskrit works like the *Puranas* (*Old World Legends*), and epic tales of the *Ramayana* and the *Mahabharata*. Socially, the rich and learned became very class-conscious. Rituals and animal sacrifices increased in the belief that gods could be appeased. And two great religious thinkers were born: Vardhamana Mahavira, a leader of Jainism, and Gautama Buddha, founder of Buddhism.

THE GREEK GIFT AND KING ASHOKA

In 327 B.C., Alexander, the Greek invader, conquered the Persian Empire and marched into Northwest India. Although Alexander's victory was temporary, the Greek contact led to an exchange of ideas between East and West for the first time.

More importantly, Greek sculpture provided the model for Indian gods and goddesses. Almost five hundred years after the Buddha's death, images of this man-turned-god were made, first with Greek features, and later in distinctly Indian styles. The Greek and Indian art forms became famous at two Buddhist centers, Gandhara and Mathura. Greek influence is therefore a landmark in the history of Indian art.

Politically, at this time, India was divided into many states, each ruled by a prince. The first king to unite the princely states and promote Buddhism both in and outside India was King Ashoka (272–236 B.C.) of the Mauryan dynasty.

Ashoka's war with the Kalinga kingdom (Orissa) proved a turning point in his life. The excessive bloodshed at the battlefield smote his conscience. Almost overnight, he became a Buddhist, spreading the message of peace and non-violence. He inscribed Buddhist principles of morality on rocks and pillars and spent his whole life doing acts of charity, helping the poor and the needy.

Buddhism spread to Sri Lanka, Central Asia and Afghanistan, thanks to Ashoka's zeal. The Ashokan pillar, now in New Delhi's museum, bears a column crowned with a four-headed lion and a *chakra* (wheel) at the center. This is India's national emblem today, signifying spiritual fearlessness and diligence.

Opposite top: **Stone sculpture of the Buddha.**

Opposite bottom: **Mahavira, a leader of Jainism.**

Below: **Four-headed lion capital of the Ashokan pillar, now a national symbol.**

GOLDEN AGE OF THE GUPTAS

After the fall of the Mauryan Empire, much of North India was disunited and fell into the hands of foreign powers—the Persians, Huns, Scythians and Sakas from Central Asia. Of these invaders, a tribe known as the Yueh Chi advanced upon the northwest frontiers and brought parts of China, Central Asia, Afghanistan and North India under a single rule. Kanishka, the Yueh Chi king, is remembered chiefly for his role in taking Buddhism into remote corners of Asia. He started the Saka era which, for a full thousand years, was used as a standard throughout Asia, just as the Christian era is today.

After a gap of more than two centuries in the political history, a strong Gupta dynasty took over India and gave the country a long period of peace and prosperity. Chandra Gupta Vikramaditya, the best known Gupta king, was a great patron of art and literature. Poet Kalidasa, the "Indian Shakespeare" born 12 centuries before the English Bard, and physician Charaka graced his court. Aryabhatta, the mathematician who discovered the use of "zero" and explained the method of calculating eclipses, also belonged to this golden age.

Many great Hindu temples and Buddhist monasteries were built in the golden age of the Guptas. Of these, the 29 Ajanta caves in Central India are the most outstanding. Carved out of solid rock, the walls and ceilings depict scenes from the Buddha's life. Ajanta cave paintings provided the inspiration for Buddhist cave paintings in Central Asia, Dun Huang caves in China and the Horyuji in Japan.

SOUTH INDIAN HISTORY

Since ancient times, South India has enjoyed greater peace and stability than the North. Tamil was and still is the language of the South. In fact, it is the oldest living language in the world today. Of the Tamil rulers, the Pallavas and Cholas have left a lasting imprint on South India. The Pallavas built the rock-cut shore temple at Mamallapuram near Madras and re-established Shiva-Vishnu worship. (Shiva and Vishnu are two Hindu gods.) The Cholas are remembered for the magnificently constructed Hindu temples and bronze sculptures found in Tanjore, Kanchi and Chidambaram in the South. They also promoted music, dance and learning throughout their united Southern Empire.

The Chola Empire extended as far south as Sri Lanka for a while, under King Rajendra Chola. He also established trade links with China via Southeast Asia. Indian culture spread to most parts of Southeast Asia from the beginning of the 4th century A.D., but especially during Chola rule, between the 8th and 11th centuries A.D. Buddhist monasteries and Hindu temples in Java, Sumatra, Malaya, Thailand and Cambodia reveal a strong Indian influence. Their language, literature, art and political systems also drew inspiration from Indian models.

From the 4th until the 9th centuries A.D., South India was the birthplace of many Tamil poet-saints who revived the people's faith in Hindu gods and goddesses. They reconverted Jain and Buddhist kings to Hinduism and wrote several poems in praise of Vishnu and Shiva. The Alwars and Nayanmars, as these poet-saints were called, were pioneers of a Hindu revivalist movement which eventually swept the whole of India. Today they are worshiped in many South Indian temples.

MEDIEVAL INDIA

While South India continued to enjoy considerable peace, North India experienced several invasions after the 9th century A.D. Indian kings remained divided and weak and could not resist Moslem attacks. Arabs, Turks, Afghans and Mongols made successive inroads into North and West India. They plundered Hindu and Buddhist places of worship, removing vast reserves of gold and jewelry. Worst of all the looting was the sacking of the famous Somnatha temple by Mahmood of Ghazni, who made away with "a great quantity of pearls, diamonds and rubies which poured out of the belly of the idol when he broke it."

The only real resistance came from the heroic and proud Rajputs of Western India. There are tales relating the courage of Rajput women who burned themselves alive rather than surrender. But even the Rajputs could not counter Moslem attacks.

It was not until the 13th century A.D. that these invaders settled down and formed a stable government. Out of political chaos rose a half-Mongol, half-Turk named Babur, whose grandson Akbar established the Mughal Empire in India.

Mamallapuram, the rock-cut shore temple in Tamil Nadu. Mamallapuram was the 7th century port city of the Pallavas, and was named after King Mamalla.

The Taj Mahal, built by Shah Jahan, has been hailed as "marbled embroidery" for its intricate workmanship. It is known as the eighth wonder of the world.

MUGHAL SPLENDOR

Akbar the Great was the first king to extend his Empire to cover the whole of North and Central India. He married a Rajput princess, showed great tolerance toward the Hindus and initiated a fusion of Hindu and Moslem art forms in architecture, painting, music and dance.

Akbar built the splendid city of Fatehpur Sikri near Delhi. It had a hall called Ibadad Khana in which people gathered to discuss various religious doctrines. He even dreamed of founding a world faith called the Din Ilahi. His son, Jehangir, was fond of landscaping Mughal gardens into replicas of a Persian paradise. Some of them can still be seen in Udaipur and Kashmir. He also loved painting, and this led to the growth of many schools of miniature painting in India.

Jehangir's son, Shah Jahan, is well remembered for the forts and mosques he constructed at enormous cost. The most outstanding is the marble mausoleum, Taj Mahal, built in loving memory of his queen, Mumtaz. The main entrance was once guarded with solid silver gates and the entire structure, inlaid with precious gems and stones, took 22 years for 22,000 workmen to complete.

With the exception of Aurangzeb, Shah Jahan's son, the Mughal kings were great lovers of music. North Indian classical dance and music—religious once—became secular, having entered the Mughal courts. The North Indian style at once became distinctly romantic, with the introduction of elements of Urdu poetry.

However, the people became poorer, especially during the cruel reign of Aurangzeb. Heavy taxes and temple funds filled the royal treasury. Landless laborers and manual workers became bonded slaves and crime increased in the countryside.

ARRIVAL OF THE EUROPEANS

Politically, the 17th century proved ripe for yet another foreign power to enter India—the British. In 1600, Queen Elizabeth I of England granted a royal charter for a group of English traders to set up a trading company, the East India Company, in the East. With a small fleet under the leadership of William Hawkins, they set up trading posts in Bombay, Madras and Calcutta.

The French, Dutch and Portuguese established their own trading centers. They bought textiles, tea, spices, gold and silver cheaply in India and sold them at an enormous profit in Europe. The European trading stations grew into flourishing cities.

The British East India Company signed treaties with various Indian princes, effectively giving the British economic advantage and political power. The fall of the Mughal Empire, the divisiveness of the Indian kings and the enterprising shrewdness of the British, backed with military might, paved the way for a British Empire in India in the 18th century.

"Jehangir's Delhi fort bears in precious inlay the proud words of a Moslem poet, "If anywhere on earth there is paradise, it is here, it is here, it is here."

BRITISH INDIA

In 1857, power was transferred from the East India Company to the British Crown and India became a British colony. After fighting a total of 111 wars in India—with Indian money and troops—British India finally saw peace and some long-lasting gains.

The British introduced modern technology. The intention was to sell manufactured goods such as textiles and machines for profit. They also built railways to make the country easy to administer and readily accessible, established factories, schools and universities and introduced the western concept of democracy. Vigorous missionary activity and the spread of Christianity in India was encouraged.

MODERN INDIA

At the start of the 20th century, some liberal British policies brought social and economic reforms. The British initiated constitutional changes, local self-government at the village level and recognized the newly formed political party, the Indian National Congress. English education opened the way for Indian intellectuals. They craved India's freedom.

The 19th century saw the growth of many political, social and religious reform movements in India. Raja Ram Mohan Roy started the Brahmo Samaj in 1828 to fight social ills such as the caste system, child marriage, superstitions and the burning of widows (*suttee*).

Ramakrishna Paramahamsa, a Hindu mystic, preached that true worship of God lies in the service of humanity. His disciple, Vivekananda, established a Hindu Order called the Ramakrishna Mission and awakened the conscience of Indians.

Vivekananda

Ram Mohan Roy

At this time, India saw the rise of a social, spiritual and political leader, Mohandas Karamchand Gandhi. He was born in 1869, became a lawyer but gave up his practice to fight for India's independence through *satyagraha*, the non-violent fight for justice.

Gandhi advised the Indians not to cooperate with the British but instead to go on peaceful strikes. He persuaded all his men to wear Indian handloom textiles instead of English cloth. He walked hundreds of miles in silent protest against a British tax on common essential items such as salt, and succeeded in its removal. Gandhi bravely went to jail time and again, making British attempts at subjugating with army might almost impossible.

India gained independence on August 15, 1947 and Jawaharlal Nehru, a leader with immense charisma, became its first Prime Minister. However, because Hindu and Moslem leaders could not overcome their differences, India was partitioned and a new nation was born—Pakistan.

India became a Republic on January 26, 1950.

Gandhi (far left), known affectionately as the "Father of the Nation," is commemorated in this monument which shows him on one of his non-violent protest marches. He was assassinated in 1948, soon after India gained independence.

GOVERNMENT

INDIA IS a sovereign socialist democratic republic and has a parliamentary system of government. Its 25 states and 7 Union Territories are governed by the Central Cabinet according to the Constitution of India, which was adopted on January 26, 1950. A state has its own government but the Union Territory comes under the government of the Central Cabinet.

The President is the Supreme head of state, elected by the Parliament for a period of five years. He is the constitutional head of the Executive, Legislature and Judiciary. The President is also the Supreme Commander of the Armed Forces, but this is only a ceremonial post. He acts on the advice of a Council of Ministers (Central Cabinet).

The Cabinet is headed by the Prime Minister. The real powers are vested with this executive body. The Central Cabinet is collectively responsible to the House of the People or the Lok Sabha. The people of India elect members to the Lok Sabha once every five years.

While executive powers rest with the Prime Minister and his Cabinet, legislative powers are given to the Parliament, which acts as a powerful forum of public opinion. The Judiciary, headed by the Chief Justice of India, protects the constitutional and statutory rights of Indian citizens.

The three powers—Executive, Legislature and Judiciary—act with one another to prevent the misuse of power. The Judiciary, for example, guards the Executive from assuming powers beyond those outlined in the Constitution.

Opposite: **A quick shine just before the parade.**

Below: **The Central Secretariat building where the Cabinet meets.**

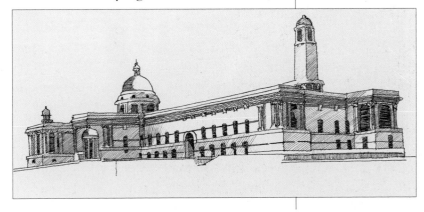

THE FEDERAL SYSTEM OF GOVERNMENT

The Constitution has provided for a federal system of government, with the government at the center and a similar structure in the states. This allows easy administration and decentralization of power.

Thus, each state has its own Governor as the constitutional head, the Chief Minister and his Council to work as the state executive, and the elected Members of the Legislative Assembly. While the government at the center covers important areas such as Defense, Foreign Affairs and Communications, the state is given autonomy in several areas, including Agriculture, Internal Law and Order, and Public Health. This power structure continues all the way down to the districts and villages.

In a similar manner, the hierarchy of the Supreme Court, High Courts, Subordinate Courts and the Panchayats (district and village courts) helps to dispense justice at various levels. To ensure uniformity, the Constitution has allowed for a single system of courts to administer both the national and the state laws.

Since there are people of different religions living in India, the Constitution has set different Personal Laws to help solve problems relating to family matters such as marriage, divorce and succession. The Hindu Marriage Act, for instance, cannot be applied to the Moslems, whose laws of marriage follow the Hanafi doctrines of Sunni Law. Similarly, different acts apply for the Christians and Parsees.

"India is a geographical and an economic entity, a cultural unity amidst diversity, a bundle of contradictions held together by strong but invisible threads."

— Pandit Jawaharlal Nehru, India's first Prime Minister.

Indira Gandhi, India's longest serving Prime Minister.

THE CONSTITUTION: A QUESTION OF RIGHTS

Many of India's national and international policies have been guided by its constitutional principles. The most important of these are the basic human rights, guaranteed by the Indian Constitution and known as the Fundamental Rights. There are six broad categories, including the right to equality, the right to freedom of speech and expression, association, assembly and movement, and the right to freedom of conscience, practice and propagation of religion. These Fundamental Rights are justiciable; any Indian citizen can fight in the courts for his Fundamental Rights.

In 1976, the Constitution was amended to include Fundamental Duties. These ensure that a citizen abides by the Constitution, defends the country in times of crisis and promotes harmony among all regions and religions.

The Constitution provides guidelines to help the government run the country. Known as the Directive Principles, they indicate that the state shall (among other things) promote the social and economic welfare of the people, improve their living and working conditions, and promote a fair distribution of wealth.

INDIA'S POLITICAL LEADERS

India's first Prime Minister, Pandit Jawaharlal Nehru, was a freedom fighter and a great statesman. He remained the unquestioned leader until his death in 1964. Representing the Congress party, which had a majority in the states as well, Nehru pursued a policy of industrialization and steered India into the modern era.

After a brief interval, his daughter, Indira Gandhi, was elected the Prime Minister. By this time, other national parties had grown to contend for leadership: the Congress party had broken into two factions; and there were several parties at the state level. West Bengal, Madras and Kerala, for example, began to have non-Congress state governments.

Mrs. Gandhi's policies were not popular with some sections of Indian society. When she declared an Emergency and suspended the Fundamental Rights, she was unseated by the people of India in the 1977 elections. Three years later, she was re-elected because of the lack of a strong alternative. In 1984, she was assassinated by a Sikh extremist.

Mrs. Gandhi's son, Rajiv Gandhi, became Prime Minister by an overwhelming majority in December 1984, but his popularity waned rapidly amidst allegations of corruption and the failure of several of his policies. In the 1989 elections, his government was unseated and the leader of an opposition party, V.P. Singh, became the new Prime Minister.

India's first Prime Minister, Pandit Jawaharlal Nehru.

ECONOMY

INDIA HAS a mixed economy. While many of its industries are owned by private enterprise, essential ones are state-owned, including manufacture of armaments, mining, transport and communications, electricity and power. Private sector companies include consumer products, textile industries and manufacture of electronics.

Successive five-year plans have helped India to achieve steady growth in gross national product, with an average annual growth of 8% in the late 1980's.

INFRASTRUCTURE, MONEY AND TRADE

A wide network of rail and road lines links all its regions, while a vast number of cargo carriers pass through India's ports. Its national airlines, Indian Airlines and Air India, help to maintain domestic and foreign air transport services.

The rupee is India's currency unit. Approximately 17 rupees equalled US$1 in October 1989. The Reserve Bank of India operates as the central bank, issuing notes and controlling the mint. All of India's major commercial and district banks are state-owned.

Although India's exports have grown considerably in the last few years, its imports are still higher than its exports, resulting in an unfavorable balance of trade. This is because of India's growing economic needs and a sharp fall in the value of the rupee.

India exports agricultural products, textile yarns and fabrics, jute, chemicals, leather goods, iron and steel, and precious stones. It imports textile fibers, petroleum products, lubricants, vegetable oils and machinery.

Opposite: **On the famous Howrah bridge in Calcutta. India's road and rail network is an essential part of its economic growth.**

Below: **Indian rupee. Note the national emblem, the lion-headed Ashokan pillar and *chakra* (wheel).**

Above: **Bio-gas plant.**

Opposite top: **Water wheel. In rural India, bullocks are still used to draw water.**

Opposite bottom: **Drying fish. Dried fish is a popular consumer product in the coastal regions.**

ENERGY

Most of India's electricity is produced using coal and petroleum products. About 40% is generated by hydro-electric power and 3% by nuclear power plants at Kota, Bombay and Kalpakkam, Madras.

India is perhaps the only country in the world to produce bio-gas with animal wastes, industrial effluents and sewage. Not only has this helped by improving sanitation, the waste by-products have been recycled even further into enriched fertilizer. In 1989, there were about 200 bio-gas plants in India.

In line with its conservation policy, India is tapping solar energy. Over 72,000 solar cookers were in use in 1987 and several solar power stations are being planned for the rural areas.

About 70% of India's energy needs are met through indigenous production. However, India still imports petroleum products for its growing energy needs from oil-producing countries including Iran, Iraq and Saudi Arabia.

AGRICULTURE

As India is primarily an agricultural country, 70% of its people are engaged in farming, and agricultural products account for two-fifths of the country's annual national product. India is self-sufficient in rice and wheat.

Although farmers in some parts of India still use the antiquated bullock-drawn plow, many have made the transition to modern farming methods, using tractors, mechanized watering, and pesticides and fertilizers. This has greatly increased grain production over the years.

However, India continues to import sugar, oil and other commodities.

MINING AND MANUFACTURING

India ranks among the leading producers of iron ore, coal and bauxite and is a significant producer of copper, mica, asbestos, chromium, gold and silver. Cotton textiles head the list of its manufactures, with jute products next in importance. Other important industries are tea-processing, petroleum refining, sugar, silks and woolens, leather products, vegetable oils, paper and electronic equipment.

Many consumer items are locally manufactured, including electrical goods, motor vehicles, television sets, videos and computers. India's software is gaining popularity in the west.

THE INDIANS

DIFFERENT STOCKS of people from Central Asia to Arabia and Greece have settled in India from time to time in the past.

It is impossible to categorize Indians of today by their racial origins but, broadly speaking, the Aryans of Indo-European stock are predominant in the North and Northwestern regions of Kashmir, Rajasthan, Punjab and Delhi. They are usually tall and fair, with pronounced features. A tribe in Ladakh known as the Drogpas is believed to be the "purest" of the Aryans living today. The Rajputs of Rajasthan may well be the descendants of the Huns of Central Asia.

The Central Indian regions of Uttar Pradesh, Madhya Pradesh and Bihar are inhabited by a mixture of Aryan and the indigenous Dravidian races. The tribal Bhils and Konds of Western and Eastern India, however, are of a purer Dravidian stock. Dark and short, the Dravidians show phenomenal resistance to the oppressive heat of the Indian summer.

A blend of the Mongoloid and Dravidian peoples live in the Eastern Indian regions of Assam, Manipur, Nagaland and Mizoram. A Tibeto-Burman type characterized by slanting eyes and high cheekbones can be found in the Himalayan foothills.

The land south of the Vindhya ranges is inhabited by a mix of Dravidians and Aryans, commonly referred to as South Indians. Purer Dravidians can still be found in the interior of the South.

Opposite: **Two Rajasthani village women.**

Below: **Modern clothes mask the regional differences of Indians.**

PEOPLE OF THE KASHMIR VALLEY

The Kashmiris and Himachalis of the North, blessed with a healthy, cold climate, are energetic, robust and exuberant at work or leisure. Moslems, Hindus and Buddhists live harmoniously in these Himalayan valleys.

Jammu is the land of warriors called Dogras and shepherd-nomads called Gujars. Both men and women of Kashmir wear *phiran* (long cloak) and *salwar* (loose pants). The women also wear a quaint headdress and large silver earrings. Moslem men wear a cap and sport a beard while Moslem women often wear a black veil, the *burkha*, which covers them completely.

In winter, Kashmiris keep warm by tucking an earthen pot of burning coal under their cloak or shawl. Known as *kangri*, the pot is fixed in a basket of cane and tied around their waist to act as a portable heater!

Kashmiris have a long established tradition of carpet and silk weaving, lacquerware and wooden handicrafts. They cultivate apples, maize and legumes in terrace fields cut out of the hills, and grow flowers and vegetables on floating rafts called *radhs*. Some live in houseboats known as *shikaras*.

Culturally, the Himachalis have much in common with the Kashmiris. In the northern plateau of Ladakh, however, live some mountain tribes, mostly Tibetan Buddhists, whose isolation has helped maintain their unique customs.

The people of the hilly regions in the North share a common love for folk arts and live in close communion with nature, reflecting a joy in life.

Opposite top: **Punjabis are a vigorous people who break into dance at any opportunity.**

Opposite bottom: **A bucket brigade clears the land for a building.**

Below: **Ladakhi spectators.**

38

PUNJABIS AND RAJASTHANIS

Punjab, known as the land of the five rivers and traditionally India's bread basket, is the most fertile state of India. The Punjabis are primarily hardworking agriculturists who grow wheat, rice, legumes and vegetables. Punjab is also known for its hosiery, woolens, sports and engineering goods.

Punjabi men wear loose white pants or the traditional Indian cloth (called *dhoti* throughout India, *tehmat* in Punjab, and *veshti*, *mundu* or *soon* in the South), a long shirt and colorful turbans. The women wear heavily embroidered long skirts or the Punjabi suit, consisting of loose pants and a long blouse. They normally cover their heads with a long scarf or a shawl. Both men and women in the countryside love to adorn themselves with jewelry.

South of Punjab is Rajasthan, the land of forts, palaces, deserts and camels. Rajasthanis are famous for handicrafts including brassware, marble work, pottery, jewelry, embroidery and painting.

Rajasthani women wear *ghagra*, wide gathered skirts which sweep the ground, and *kanchli* (embroidered blouses). They cover their heads and faces with brightly printed veils called *odhni* and adorn themselves with very heavy ornaments.

Rajasthani men wear loose *dhoti* or *churidar* (tight pants) and a waistcoat with a distinctive cut. They usually sport impressively huge moustaches and colorful turbans. Warm and good-natured, the people of Rajasthan take pride in their simplicity, honesty and thrifty habits, the latter being almost proverbial among all Indians.

PEOPLE OF INDIA'S HEARTLAND

The Northern and Central Indian states of Uttar Pradesh, Madhya Pradesh and Bihar are the most densely populated regions of India. The heartland's rich mineral wealth has given rise to iron and steel industries, oil refineries, chemical plants, fertilizer factories and paper industries in these states.

The rural people of India's heartland are primarily agriculturists who grow sugarcane, wheat, rice and lentils. They rely heavily on the rivers Ganges and Yamuna for their livelihood, apart from the rain-fed rivers of Son, Ken and Betwa.

Primitive tribes of the Bastar hills and the Chattisgarh plains live in Madhya Pradesh, hunting and working in forests, while the tribes in Chota Nagpur, Bihar are farmers practicing archaic methods of cultivation. The Central Indian belt has one notorious feature—its dacoits, professional robbers adept at traversing the treacherous terrain on horseback.

Men and women in Central India wear lighter clothes, mainly because of the heat. The women wear elaborate jewelry, as do women all over India; jewelry represents savings that can be pawned or sold in an emergency. Only a widow abstains from any form of ornamentation.

This Hindi speaking belt is also known as the "pious heartland." Several religious centers such as Varanasi, Badrinath, Prayag and Mathura are located here.

THE EAST AND THE ASSAMESE

The Eastern regions of Assam, Meghalaya, Nagaland, Manipur, Tripura and Arunachal Pradesh are inhabited by several tribes. The Khasis, Garos, Jaintias, Mundas, Nagas, Ahoms, Bodos, Miris and Wanchos are some of them. Each tribe has its own language, customs and dress. The land is covered by dense hilly jungle and marshland, rich in mineral deposits. The people have learned to adapt their lifestyle to the extremities of climate and soil conditions. Because of the marshes, houses are built on hilltops with bamboo, unlike the mud-and-thatch huts in other parts of India. Houses in Assam stand above ground on wooden poles for added protection against heavy rains and insects.

Rice is the chief crop cultivated, and the Assamese are also great tea growers. Pineapples, oranges and bananas are abundant in this part of India. Bamboo work, cane products and weaving are important cottage industries, and every home has a weaving loom so the women can supplement the family income.

The women in Mizoram and Nagaland wear a tight *sarong* wound like a dress. In Assam, they wear a *mekhela* (long skirt) and *retir* (blouse). Both men and women of the hunting tribe of Nagas in Nagaland wear jewelry made of bone, shell and horn.

Women play a larger role than men in the fields and at home. They sing and dance on every occasion, and in this they are like most other Indians. The Hindus of the East are mostly worshipers of Shakti, the fertility goddess. Culturally, they have much in common with their Burmese and Nepalese neighbors.

Top: **Naga warrior. "Naga" is a comprehensive term describing various Tibeto-Burmese tribes of India. Nagas were once headhunters.**

Bottom: **People of the Eastern states.**

BENGALIS, SIKKIMESE AND ORIYAS

Calcutta, the capital city in West Bengal vibrant with lovers of literature, music and other arts, has its unfortunate side. It is an example of the gaping disparity between the very rich and the very poor. Calcutta's poor are homeless pavement dwellers who lead a miserable existence on the roads and bridges of the city. Poverty has driven them to steal and beg. Yet Calcutta is also where some of India's wealthiest Bengalis reside.

Many Bengalis in the countryside are engaged in farming and fishing. They live in huts with sloping thatch roofs. Men wear *dhoti* and a *kurtha* (long shirt) while women wear *sari*, usually white with a colored border. Bengalis love to decorate the floor at the entrance to their homes with traditional designs called *alpana*.

North of West Bengal is the tiny Himalayan state of Sikkim, inhabited by Lepchas, Bhutias and Nepalese. They wear colorful handwoven dresses, drink yak's milk and grow fruits, potatoes, cardamom and barley.

Orissa, south of West Bengal and Bihar, is famous for its sculptured temples, dance, painting and silver filigree. Well-endowed with rivers, it is a fertile coastal plain with large groves of coconut, mango and palm, and fields of rice and sugarcane. Mining and jute growing are other important occupations.

Opposite top: **In Calcutta, the capital city of West Bengal, a street boy gets ready to brew his tea on a charcoal stove.**

Below: **A middle-aged Bengali couple. The man is dressed in *dhoti* and *kurtha*.**

South Indians gathered at a communal well.

SOUTH INDIANS IN THE LAND OF TEMPLES

South India's magnificent temples are not mere legacies of a bygone era but a living, thriving tradition. They have helped the people of the Southern states to retain their heritage.

South Indians are a blend of Dravidian groups and Aryans. They are the Tamils of Tamil Nadu, the Telugus of Andhra Pradesh, the Malayalees of Kerala, the Kannadigas of Karnataka and the Tulus of the Malabar coast.

In the countryside, Southern Indian men wear a small *dhoti* that resembles a loincloth. Often they are bare-chested and walk barefoot. The women wear a *sari* with a short blouse. Elderly women, with earlobes stretched by heavy earrings, often wear no blouse, covering themselves deftly with a *sari* instead.

The farmers grow mainly rice, sugarcane and coconuts. Some villages specialize in weaving, pottery, metal casting and stone sculpting.

People in the Southern cities reflect a mixed taste for modern and traditional values; one may see women in *sari*, their hair decked with flowers, going to work in a modern office. Classical music or dance lessons for every girl child is the norm, while great importance is attached to education, especially in Kerala, the city with the highest rate of literacy in India.

WESTERN INDIANS

The people of Gujarat, Goa and Maharashtra are a mixture of Dravidian and Aryan races, Parsees who originally came from Persia, Portuguese of mixed descent, and Caucasians who settled in Western Indian ports.

Gujarati villagers grow rice, wheat, maize, sugarcane, cotton, groundnuts and sunflower seeds. The women wear a heavily embroidered long skirt and a short blouse, and their heads are generally covered with a long cloth. Gujarati men, especially from Kutch, wear tight white pants, gathered near the ankles. Their colorful and rather unique waistcoat is now a pan-Indian fashion.

Women of a Goan hill tribe.

Maharashtra's hilly Western Ghats are very fertile, being fed by a number of rivers. Rice, groundnuts, tobacco and the famous "Alphonso" mangoes are cultivated, in addition to cotton, the main crop. Rural Maharashtrian women tie their *sari* trouser-style, and wear huge nose rings that dangle right down to the chin! The Goans and the people of Daman and Diu islands wear a knee-length *sari* as well as the western skirt and blouse. Many men have discarded traditional clothes for shirts and trousers.

Bombay, the capital city of Maharashtra known as the Gateway of India, is the country's most important industrial city, besides being its biggest port and the nerve center of India's business and finance. Bombay is also the country's largest film making center. Bombayites are cosmopolitan and many adopt a western lifestyle and outlook. The city has distinct Maharashtrian, Gujarati, Parsee, Tamil and Sindhi colonies.

LIFESTYLE

SOCIETY AND ITS PERCEPTIONS

IN A TRADITIONAL society such as India, change comes last and least to the village. Life is a regular pattern of sowing, reaping, praying and celebrating at family or social gatherings. These simple, repetitive acts acquire a symbolic meaning.

The family plays a vital role in the process. An Indian family is usually a home of three generations, rooted in a particular community. The family is also where traditional arts, crafts or a trade is learned and passed down. The collectiveness of the family fosters a strong sense of belonging—and "belonging" is a serious and exacting concern in India. The family belongs to a particular lineage (*gotra*), is identified with a particular clan (*jati*) within a specific caste of a region (*kula*). Through marriage, usually planned by collective choice over individual preference, families strengthen their bonds of lineage.

In a village, a man may be leaving for the city to better his prospects or to further his education, but the family connections are seldom lost—at least for now!

Opposite: **Indian women on a barefoot journey to a festival.**

Below: **Three-generation family units are the norm.**

An arranged marriage to strengthen bonds of lineage is as intricate an affair as trying to match differently shaded embroidery threads. A man from the priestly Brahmin caste could, for instance, be an *Iyer* or an *Iyengar*, depending on whether he is a follower of Shiva or Vishnu. If he is an *Iyengar*, he could belong to a *Vadagalai* or a *Tengalai* subgroup (Northern or Southern culture group). He would seek his lineage from a particular *rishi* or sage such as *Bharadwaja* or *Srivatsa gotra*. Why? That's another story!

THE PATRIARCHAL SYSTEM

In most Indian families, the father has ultimate authority in the home. He loves the fuss made over him by members of the household and makes decisions that may not reflect his wife's choice. The woman's role is often reduced to cooking and nurturing children.

The father, more than the mother, exerts control over the children. At times, the overpowering influence continues even when a son has grown into adulthood, with the father making important family decisions for as long as he lives.

Before 1955, when the Hindu Marriage Act legalized monogamy, a man could have more than one wife. In many remote villages, polygamy exists and goes unnoticed. Polygamy (marriage to more than one woman at the same time) is legal only among Indian Moslems.

A Maharaja receives the good wishes of his visitors. The princely caste still commands great respect.

Indians prefer a male child as Hindu rituals require a male to fulfill obligations to the ancestors. Double standards still exist for boys and girls in and outside the home. Families would much rather send sons than daughters for higher studies, for example, and unequal access to professional jobs in favor of males is the norm. No wonder the Indian male is reluctant to change with the times.

Change is coming, however, though slowly. Industrialization, equal educational opportunities for those women who care to benefit from it, and exposure to western ideas have shaken the mastery of the Indian male, at least in the cities.

THE CASTE SYSTEM

The caste system, which divided society into distinct social groups, was the most abused of all social institutions in India, and its legacy is still apparent in many regions. While the system gave order to life and prescribed a code of conduct for all, it created vast social disparities and resulted in exploitation of the underprivileged.

Brahmins had access to knowledge and became the social and intellectual elite of India. The illiterate millions were divided into some three thousand sub-castes, which were actually industrial guilds. The lowest order of scavengers, sweepers and butchers were the social "out-castes" known as Untouchables. Gandhi called them "Harijan"— Children of God."

Hindu priest reading a religious book.

The government pays special attention to the needs of economically backward groups, yet caste-consciousness is difficult to erase. In some villages, the Harijans are still barred from drawing water at public wells or entering the inner sanctum of a temple.

Caste is considered when it comes to marriage, especially in the South. Brahmins will marry only within their caste and so it is with Chettiar moneylenders of the South or the royalty of Rajasthan. Love marriages between castes are on the increase in cities, however.

Caste discrimination is on the wane, but the caste identification lingers on. Neighborhoods, lifestyles, food habits, speech patterns, dress styles and surnames reveal caste and lineage easily, and this perpetuates the old system.

CHANGING FACES OF WOMEN

Women in some Dravidian societies, especially in Kerala in the South and Manipur in the East, enjoy considerable freedom and equality. It is common for Kerala women to marry and "bring home" their husbands, and property can pass from mother to daughter. The Metei women of Assam also command a greater socio-economic status than their Indian sisters. Priestesses exist in the Assamese tradition.

In the fast-changing cities, the role of the working woman is a paradox. Economic independence and the popular women's liberation movement have given Indian women a new sense of freedom and confidence. But heavy demands on her at work and at home have also given rise to conflicts, increasing the rate of divorce.

Purdah, a system where women could not even talk to men without a veil or screen between them, is almost non-existent. Child marriage is virtually absent. *Suttee*, a medieval practice where widows were burned alive on their husband's funeral pyre, has disappeared and more women are re-marrying every year. A number of women's periodicals discuss the most modern issues from fashion to premarital sex and drugs. Women vote and hold important political positions. Most city women are graduates, many of them doctors, professors and lawyers.

Nonetheless, cooking and childcare are still the woman's responsibility. Dowry in arranged marriages is still expected, if not demanded of the bride's family. Indians are far from achieving equality of the sexes.

Women earning a modest income, packaging spices in a small factory.

Schoolchildren on an excursion.

INDIAN CHILDHOOD

The moment of birth is marked with an astrological calendar and the child's horoscope is charted. If it is a son, he will inherit the family skills and honor the household gods. If it is a daughter, she will in time teach her children the family traditions.

On the eleventh day after birth, or a few days later in some communities, the child is dressed in finery and blessed with a name. The name is written on a mound of paddy (unhusked rice) or wheat, and the baby is placed on it for a while. Only then is the child believed to have overcome afterbirth complications. For Indians, human birth has an analogy with plant life and a successful birth is likened to a successful harvest.

Every milestone from then on is a rite to be performed, an occasion celebrated, whether it is weaning from breastmilk, the first step, ear piercing, head shaving, or the first birthday. Astrologically auspicious times are selected for celebrations.

The first step towards formal education is significant. The Hindus call it *Vidyarambha*, the Moslems, *Bismillah*. In the Islamic tradition, the

Maulvi or priest helps the child recite a Koranic text and solemnizes formal learning.

In orthodox Hindu groups, the boy's initiation is as vital as his entry into studenthood. The thread ceremony (*Upanayanam*) among three upper castes—Warrior, Priest and Merchant—symbolizes spiritual rebirth. Amid Vedic chants, the boy undergoes rites to cleanse his body and mind, and is given three sacred threads to wear across his shoulders for the rest of his life.

The Hindu girl does not go through a formal initiation. In many Dravidian societies, however, the first period is celebrated with feasting and there is talk in the air of an impending marriage.

Ear piercing is common for both boys and girls. The custom originated long ago, when knowledge was transmitted orally. Piercing the ear was believed to sharpen the child's hearing and increase the mental retention capacity.

TRADITIONAL MARRIAGE

Orthodox Hindus believe that an unmarried man or woman has no social status. A Hindu marriage is a life-long partnership, a sacred and unalterable union. Rarely is a traditional marriage entrusted to the whims of the boy or girl. Their parents fix the alliance after consulting the astrologers, matching horoscopes and comparing castes, status and family backgrounds.

The marriage ceremony itself is rich in symbolism, and preparations begin weeks before the event. Ritual practice may vary in detail from region to region, but the Vedic ritual itself has remained unchanged for more than two thousand years.

Constructing a temporary altar for the fire god, the priest acts as Brahma. The bride and groom are also likened to Indian gods and goddesses: Shiva and Shakti, or Vishnu and Lakshmi. The marriage is complete when the groom ties a sacred thread called *mangala sutra* around the bride's neck, the couple walks around the fire, and blessings are received from all the elders present.

The union is sanctified, making divorce unthinkable in the Indian tradition. There is no equivalent for the word "divorce" in the dictionary of any of the Indian languages! *Talaq*, meaning "divorce," is used freely in Hindi, but it is an Arabic term imported by the Moslems.

Newspaper advertisement for a bride. The daily is a modern matchmaker.

MATRIMONIAL

Alliance invited for Haritasa, Telugu Aruvela Niyogi Brahmin groom 31. A science and law graduate, currently working at Saudi and desirous of migrating to USA/Canada. As advt. is for wider choice interested parents/guardians are requested to respond soonest alongwith horoscope details etc., to:

Bride and groom on a swing constructed especially for the occasion.

MODERN MARRIAGE

In the cities, long years of formal education have pushed up the marriageable age to the late twenties and thirties. To family considerations are added the preference of the young people and educational or professional compatibility. When traditional yardsticks are to be used for matchmaking, Indian newspapers act as efficient "go-betweens" by carrying classified advertisements in their special matrimonial columns.

In some societies, dowry is expected and accepted, although it is an out-dated tradition and a legally punishable offense. In a few extreme cases in the North, there have been incidents of wife-beating, even wife-burning, when financial expectations have not been met by the bride's family.

Some modern families do not mind inter-caste, inter-regional or even inter-religious marriages, when the man and the woman have known each other for years, either at college or in their workplace. Some prefer to remain single, while a handful even experiment with living together without a formal commitment.

Today's educated Indians modernize the external forms of marriage by holding receptions at five-star hotels while retaining the basic Vedic ritual. Change on the one hand, tradition on the other.

The most important marriage chant goes: "Take seven steps with me, my friend. Be my mate and blend with me."

OLD AGE: BOON OR CURSE?

Ageing is a beautiful stage of life in traditional India. When the son marries and adds to the family community, the parents move up the ladder of seniority and are consulted on all important family matters. In due course, even the neighbors and friends seek their blessings on all auspicious occasions.

In ancient times, when a man and his wife became old, they were expected to give up the materialistic family life and settle in a forest, practicing a simple, spiritual way of life. Today, although the elderly do not proceed to the forest, they make pilgrimages to religious centers and gradually relegate mundane home affairs to the younger generation. Seldom is there a clash of interest between the old and the new; where resentment exists, it is rarely revealed, out of deference for old age.

The cities, however, present a slightly different picture. Younger family members prefer to set up their own homes, either to be nearer their workplace or because the joint family structure no longer appeals to them. Families meet only during festivals and family celebrations. Retirees feel less inclined to rely on their children, and a growing number save for their future. But though they are more self-reliant financially, the aged in the cities are less prepared emotionally. They face very real problems of loneliness, due to the breakdown of the extended family.

THE HINDU VIEW OF LIFE AND DEATH

To the Hindu, life is a ceaseless cycle of events which begins where it ends. Death is merely a stage in that chain, as inevitable as birth itself. Therefore, death is not final, just a transfer of the soul from one body to another, quite like casting off old clothes to wear new ones.

Whether one reappears in the next life as a plant, an insect, an animal or a human, and whether it is a happy and prosperous life or a troubled existence, depend on actions performed in previous lives. It is believed that a truly noble life, with good thoughts, words and deeds, would release the soul from the life cycle and secure eternal liberation, called *moksha*. (Buddhists call this *nirvana*.)

While a Hindu performs several rites during his lifetime, surviving relatives perform last rites for his well-being in the next life. Failure to perform them would cause his soul to wander without a place in the next world.

The eldest son usually performs last rites with the help of a priest. The body is dressed in new clothes, placed on a bier and taken to the cremation grounds amid the chanting of God's name. The pyre is lit and the ashes are collected the next day for immersion in the holy river. Thirteen days of mourning begin, to be completed with a ritual and a feast, both of which suggest a return to normalcy.

Although cremation is the norm among Hindus, young children and persons held in very great reverence are buried, and so also are Moslems and Christians. Victims of epidemics are generally cast away in water so as not to offend the "evil spirits" that have attacked the victim.

"Life is a stage with one entrance and many exits."

KARMA, THE GUIDING PRINCIPLE

Karma is a fundamental belief among Indians. It means "action." Like the principle of cause and effect, good turns fetch a reward of good life while bad words and deeds affect not just this life but the next as well. Logically, therefore, a man's birth in this life is determined by the cumulative good or bad actions of his previous lives.

Karma offers explanations for the inequalities of life—such as why a man is born poor or handicapped or suffers a series of hardships while another, even if born to the same family, enjoys peace and prosperity. *Karma* blames man himself, not God, for his state of poverty or ignorance.

Belief in *karma* has generally made the Indian passively accept his state of poverty. Although *karma* does not mean a fatalistic pessimism, the man in the countryside will always talk of his *karma*, whether his crops fail or his son fails! It allows him to face without flinching those hardships he cannot avert.

Indians also believe that stars and planets affect the individual, and that the elements of earth, water, fire, wind and space rule man's health and well-being. Many of their beliefs have foundation in the ancient sciences of astrology and medicine. In Indian society, where faith involves belief in the supernatural and myths are still alive, they often get mixed with strange superstitions.

SUPERSTITIONS

If superstitions are caused by man's fear of the unknown, it explains why they are an integral part of any traditional society. Indians may use the Gregorian calendar for their daily transactions but when it comes to buying property, starting on a venture or even moving house, they go by the Indian astrological calendar. In this, even numbers are regarded as auspicious or inauspicious. Generally, 8 and 9 are good while 7 is not. Wednesday is good for traveling and Friday auspicious for sacred matters. On Friday, meat is taboo, a visit to the barber's frowned upon and visiting the home of the bereaved simply out of the question!

Some of these may be "customs and beliefs," but the label "superstition" takes over when meaning is attached to events beyond human control. For instance, if a person sneezes before a project starts, it will not be completed; if a lizard falls on one's head, death is imminent; if a dog howls in the neighborhood, it is the call of Yama, the god of death. The list is endless.

No one really knows how some of these superstitions came about, but the epic *Mahabharata* refers to creatures of ill omen. The *Puranas* tell frightening tales of what befalls those who do not believe in ancient practices.

These old stories also prescribe antidotes. Thus, bathing in the holy river to wash away one's sins, and offering one's hair to the Lord as a symbol of sacrifice may appear superstitious to some, but are religious obligations for the millions living in India.

Fortuneteller with a client. Astrologers and fortunetellers are part of the fabric of Indian society.

SOME TRIBAL CUSTOMS

Opposite top: **Water pots have to be filled at the communal village well.**

Opposite bottom: **Village women weave cloth for their own use as well as to supplement the family income.**

Below: **Tribal dance before going for the hunt.**

Quite apart from the city dweller or the villager lives the tribal Indian whose customs reveal his intimate relationship with the "spirits." Whether it is to seek a good harvest or to cure an illness, the entire community is pressed into service for the primitive magical rituals.

Using mystical and sometimes occult powers, they resort to sorcery and witchcraft to purify wayward souls and victims of the "evil eye." The entire community is quarantined if untimely deaths or epidemics occur. Along with strict taboos for several days, rituals are performed by witch-doctors to appease high-ranking spirits and return the evil to its initiators.

Spirits could reside in trees, plants, hills, springs, iron implements, diseases such as smallpox and chickenpox—almost anything the tribe fears or reveres. Specialist mediums are believed to remove the curse of evil by communicating with the spirits through trances and divination.

Sacrifices may be offered. To satisfy the earth's demands, the Konds of Central India make ritual sacrifices to the earth goddess, Tari. What used to be a human sacrifice a hundred years ago is now replaced by strips of buffalo flesh buried in the soil to ensure fertility.

Although the tribes are slowly modernizing through education and social interaction, many prefer their isolation.

LIFE IN THE VILLAGES

Village life anywhere in India is similar, despite regional differences. Men and women wake up when dawn breaks and go to the pond, river or backyard well to clean themselves. They chew twigs of the Neem tree to clean their teeth, or use forefingers and tooth powder to wash their mouth. A quick bath in cold water, then clothes are washed by beating them on rough stone and scrubbing with soap. On special days, especially in the South, oil is massaged all over the body and rinsed with indigenous herbs and powders.

Coffee is the beverage of the South while tea is standard in the North. Seated on the floor, they eat either food left over from the previous night's meal, or drink rice, millet or wheat porridge. Then the men proceed to the fields or workplace, children to schools and women to fetch water or firewood.

Everybody returns before sunset to attend to the cows and goats in their sheds, play traditional games, watch village shows or attend temple festivals. There is plenty of leisure time for entertainment and social interaction. Evenings are for gossiping about politics or village affairs. Then, spreading the mat on the floor to sleep, they retire after checking that the animals have been fed and the water pots filled for the next day's chores.

LIFE IN THE CITIES

City life presents many sharp contrasts. Apart from the wealth and poverty revealed by the coexistence of luxury bungalows and slums, the city centers are generally congested.

Heavy demand and limited supply have created shortages of various kinds, from housing, water, electricity and telephones to transport facilities, school and college admissions, and employment opportunities. Many Indians seek employment abroad; many middle-class women have also joined the workforce. More money to spend has led to growing consumerism.

Yet, life in Indian cities can be rewarding. The people are caring and warm. Whether it is reaching out to a neighbor or extending hospitality to a stranger, Indians respond readily, almost instinctively.

Urban dwellers are increasingly becoming lovers of Indian classical art, turning the cities culturally vibrant with music and dance festivals that last several weeks in some seasons. The growth of art institutions reflects a surging interest in art among Indian youths. It has even become fashionable to use ethnic textiles and folk crafts. All seems bright for India's age-old traditions.

Seats on the bus—literally. This is child's play to the seasoned train traveler who may see not only rooftop passengers, but also vendors selling their wares!

Opposite: Bicycles and scooters are common means of transport besides public buses. Cars, trucks, rickshaws and bullock carts often move together on narrow streets, increasing travel time and risk of accidents.

63

RELIGION

INDIA IS a secular country and Indians are free to practice the faith of their choice. Assimilation of various religious values have made the Indians generally very tolerant. However, religious unrest is not uncommon, especially in recent years, when politics has exploited religious differences.

All the major religions of the world have found a home in India, itself the birthplace of two major religions: Hinduism and Buddhism. Hindus form nearly 80% of the population, the remaining 20% consisting of Moslems, Christians, Sikhs, Buddhists, Jains, Jews and Zoroastrians.

Religion plays an important part in the life of Indians on the whole. Almost every joyous occasion is celebrated with a visit to a shrine because Indians love to go on pilgrimages. And virtually every day of the year marks a festive occasion associated with one faith or another. Religious processions are undertaken not just by Hindus but also by Moslems, Christians and Buddhists.

Each religious community displays symbols of its faith at the main door to invoke the protection of the gods upon the household. The Christian, for example, adorns it with the cross or the flaming heart, the Moslem with a verse from the Koran, and the Hindu with a picture of Ganesha, the god who wards off evil.

Opposite: **The Bahai temple in India. Bahai has Persian roots. Freedom to practice any religion is a Fundamental Right in India.**

Left: **Prayer at dawn on the ghats by the river Ganges in Varanasi.**

HINDUISM

Hinduism is the oldest living faith in the world and forms the ethos of the majority of Indians. It is important to understand the religion in order to understand the Indians, particularly as Hinduism is more a way of life than a religion.

Unlike many other faiths, Hinduism does not have a founder, nor is it based on any single scripture. Indians call it *Sanatana Dharma*—the faith with no beginning and no end.

Hinduism offers different approaches to persons of different aptitudes. It does not prescribe rules. Rather, it reveals profound "truths" about life and suggests various paths of righteous living. As the choice of path is left to Hindus, the religion means different things to different people. Yet, one can understand certain aspects of the religion by examining some of its essential features, starting with the *Vedas*. These are sacred texts containing hymns of creation, prayers and philosophical discussions. They are chanted on every auspicious or solemn occasion.

To simplify high philosophy and offer it to the common man, legends were created. The *Puranas*, the *Ramayana* and the *Mahabharata* are stories that drive home universal values of righteous living. A part of the *Mahabharata* is the *Bhagavad Gita*, a philosophical *Song of God* that brings out the essence of Hinduism in simple form. Here, Lord Krishna advocates three paths: the path of mental discipline to the intellectual; the pursuit of love and devotion to the emotional; and the path of selfless service to those who believe that "work is worship." And to all, he advocates the virtues of non-violence, truth and detachment.

Opposite top: **Aum, the primeval sound.**

Opposite bottom: **Hindu priest blesses devotees.**

Below: **A monumental and intricately carved** *gopuram* **or gateway to a Hindu temple.**

HINDU VALUES

Hinduism does not deny one the enjoyment of life. It advocates the pursuit of four goals: *dharma, artha, kama* and *moksha.* These translate roughly as righteous living, wealth and prosperity, love and happiness, and finally, release from the cycle of births and deaths.

A Hindu must pursue the right action at the right time. Thus a man's life is roughly divided into four stages: childhood, joyous and innocent; student life, disciplined in mind and body; householder, married with a family; and renunciation of material things in preparation for the final years. Since these stages are common to all, Hindu priests also marry and raise a family.

Hindu gods and goddesses reflect the Hindu value system. Anything beautiful, valuable or awesome is associated with divinity. Plant and animal life, natural forces of energy, the sun, planets, the elements, art, knowledge, wealth and happiness—all have their corresponding deities.

Amid this host of gods and goddesses is the concept of the Hindu Trinity: Brahma the Creator, Vishnu the Preserver, and Shiva the Destroyer. Together, they symbolize the Ultimate God known as Brahman, represented with the formless sound symbol, *Aum.* (*Brahman* should not be confused with the priestly caste known as *Brahmin.*)

Although Hindus believe that all these gods are different manifestations of one Supreme God, the deities are very real to them; their birthdays and marriage anniversaries are great occasions for celebration in homes and in temples. Hinduism really comes alive during such festivals.

HINDU RITUALS AND BELIEFS

Rituals are a part of the Hindu way of life. From the time of conception until death, a Hindu observes various ceremonies in order to achieve total development. Although some of the customs are now obsolete, many are followed to this day. They are imbued with rich symbolism, each a prayer for prosperity and offspring in this life and in the next.

The cow is holy to the Hindu, who worships her as the Divine Mother; therefore, beef is taboo. The cow is the source of life-sustaining milk and also the symbol of fertility. Every animal, in fact, is associated with a god: the elephant with Ganesha, the snake with Vishnu, the bull with Shiva, the peacock with Murugan, the swan with Brahma and so on. This association of gods with animals is one of the reasons why many Hindus are vegetarians. Some refrain from meat by choice, others because of caste considerations.

Water is sacred to Hindus and many pious Hindus feel blessed after a dip in the river, particularly the Ganges. Most temples also have a pond in the courtyard for bathing.

During the Ganapati festival in Western India and Durga Puja in Bengal, huge images of deities are installed and consecrated. This is known as the life-giving ceremony. After ten days of prayers and offerings, they are taken on a procession and ceremonially immersed in the river, pond or sea, suggesting a renewal and a rebirth for the gods.

BUDDHISM

Buddhism, founded by Gautama Buddha in the 6th century B.C., spread across the whole of Asia but was eclipsed from Indian soil as a distinct religion sometime around the 12th century A.D. Many of its ways were absorbed into Hinduism where Buddha became one of the incarnations of the Hindu god, Vishnu.

The early 20th century saw a revival movement led by Dr. B.R. Ambedkar, as a result of which there are more than four million Buddhists in India today. The majority of them live in Maharashtra in Western India. The Himalayan regions of Ladakh and Leh, however, have remained Buddhist since ancient times.

Buddhism stands on three pillars: Buddha, its founder; Dharma, his teachings; and Sangha, the order of monkhood. The essence of Buddhism lies in the "Four Noble Truths" and the "Eightfold Path." Buddha preached that desire is the root of all suffering, and that detachment and freedom from desire can lead to higher wisdom. The "Eightfold Path" is in correct understanding, thought, speech, action, livelihood, effort, mind and meditation. Following this path, the Buddhist can free himself of ignorance, control his senses and attain *nirvana*, or release from the cycle of births and deaths.

Buddhism was divided into three distinct schools a few centuries after Gautama Buddha. The Theravada or the Original sect is practiced in India, Burma, Sri Lanka and Thailand. The easier-to-follow Mahayana sect is popular in Tibet, China, Korea and Japan. Vajrayana is an esoteric offshoot of Mahayana which introduced magic, mysticism and the worship of male-female union. Japanese Zen is the meditative aspect of Buddhism, known as Dhyana.

Opposite: **This Jain woman, just before she becomes a nun, is dressed as a bride. The cloth taped across her mouth prevents her from destroying insects.**

Below: **Two Buddhist novices rest in a shelter.**

JAINISM

"Jina" means one who has conquered the senses. It is the name given to Vardhamana Mahavira, the great reformer and religious leader who lived during Buddha's time. His followers are known as Jains, or those who practice control of the senses. Although Jainism developed earlier than Buddhism and spread throughout South India, today it has just about three million followers among the merchant communities of Gujarat, Uttar Pradesh and Rajasthan.

The Jains have contributed substantially to the social and cultural life of India in the past. Many Hindu practices, such as vegetarianism and fasting, are Jain in origin. Jains adhere to strict physical and mental discipline. Through a rigorous code of morality, self-denial and non-violence, they strive to achieve salvation. To this day, orthodox Jains will not eat onions and garlic, which are said to increase sensual desires, and they abstain from fermented edibles for fear of harming living bacteria.

The Jains have merged with the Hindu community. They intermarry, worship Lakshmi, the Hindu goddess of wealth, and celebrate Hindu festivals as well as Mahavir Jayanti, Mahavira's birthday. Their religious symbol is the swastika, which is considered auspicious by Hindus and Buddhists as well.

There are two main sects of Jainism: the Swetambaras who worship Mahavira in white robe, and the Digambaras who portray their god completely naked. A huge statue of unadorned Mahavira stands majestically at Sravanabelagola in Mysore.

Golden Temple of Amritsar with a good view of the *sarovar* (holy water tank) around it.

SIKHISM

The term "Sikh" is derived from the Sanskrit word *shiksh*, which means "to learn." In Punjabi, it refers to a learner or a disciple. The followers of Guru Nanak and his nine spiritual successors have come to be known as Sikhs. The Gurus' sayings and verses are found in the holy book of Guru Granth Sahib, which Sikhs venerate in their homes and *gurdwaras* (temples).

Guru Nanak, the founder teacher of Sikhism, was born in 1469 in a village called Talwandi Rai Bhoe, now in Pakistan. Guru Nanak was spiritual even as a young boy, rejecting caste and religious distinctions and preaching the doctrine of One God, which he simply called Ikk ("One"). He felt that God could be perceived through loving devotion.

Sikhism grew into an institution only under the fifth teacher, Guru Arjan, in the 16th century. He constructed the Harimandir—the Golden

Temple at Amritsar, the holiest shrine of the Sikhs today. His successor, Guru Hargobind, adorned himself with two swords and gave a martial direction to Sikhism. Within a century thereafter, Sikhism had become a cohesive social and political force.

Sikh men carry certain common features: their turban which covers hair left uncut from birth, a beard, a steel bangle, a knife and a special undergarment. They are believed to make good warriors due to a fearless tenacity, amply indicated by their surname, Singh, which means "lion."

Culturally, Sikhs are like the Hindus of the Punjab region and intermarriage used to be common. Since 1980, however, tension between them has been mounting, with an extremist group calling for an independent Sikh homeland, Khalistan—Land of the Pure.

Sikh devotees inside the Golden Temple of Amritsar.

Above: **Moslem men prostrate themselves in prayer in a street of Bombay.**

Opposite: **Home for the destitute. The Norwegian 20th century saint of India, Mother Teresa, and her Christian mission have provided a haven for thousands of destitutes and lepers.**

ISLAM

Islam was imported into India by Moslem conquerors and Arab merchants in the 10th century A.D. Many Hindus were forced into conversion; some were offered economic incentives as a reward; others were drawn into Islam by its high ideal of universal brotherhood.

Islam is an Arabic term that means both "submission to God" and "peace." Its founder, Prophet Mohammed, was born in Mecca in the 6th century A.D. Moslems believe that divine messages came to him from God, and that these are collected in the sacred book, the Koran.

Every Moslem has to follow certain basic principles enshrined in the Koran. He must profess his faith in Allah, the one ultimate God, recite prayers five times a day, fast during the month of Ramadan, give a part of his wealth to charity and go on a Haj (pilgrimage to Mecca) at least once in his lifetime if he can afford it.

Although Islam spread across nearly all regions, India's Moslem population is concentrated in Uttar Pradesh, parts of Gujarat, Bengal, Kashmir, Kerala, Hyderabad and Tamil Nadu. They are mainly merchants, artists and artisans but are spread in other sectors of the economy as well.

There are two main Islamic sects: Shia and Sunni. Indian Moslems are mostly Sunni. Some practice Sufism, a mystical doctrine that emphasizes direct communion with God through intuitive knowledge.

CHRISTIANITY

The history of Christianity in India presents an interesting study, since its 15 million adherents belong to several Christian groups and churches, brought into India by missionaries at different times. About 4 million belong to the Church of St. Thomas, the apostle who is believed to have arrived in Cochin, South India, in the 1st century A.D., to spread the message of Jesus Christ. Followers of the St. Thomas Church are known as Syrian Christians.

The arrival of the Portuguese in Goa and the French in Pondicherry in the medieval period brought fresh directions to Catholicism in these parts. The 18th and 19th centuries, during which the British entrenched themselves in India, saw the spread of English Protestantism, mainly in East India, through educational and charitable institutions. Marriages between Indians and Europeans also resulted in an ethnic subgroup of Christian Anglo-Indians in this era.

Today, there are Christians in all sections of society. While many Christians in the cities of Bombay and Calcutta have adopted western values and culture, the South Indian Christians, particularly in the suburbs and villages, can hardly be distinguished from their Hindu neighbors, for they share one another's customs and beliefs.

ZOROASTRIANISM

Zoroastrianism has its name from its founder, Zoroaster, a Persian prophet who pondered over life and existence and realized that absolute energy lies in perfect wisdom which he called Ahura Mazda. His followers are known as Zoroastrians.

Preceding all other philosophies in India, it influenced the Indo-Aryan Vedic philosophy in the early periods, although it was only in the 8th century A.D. that a group of Persian Zoroastrians, persecuted by Moslems in their own land, set sail towards Kathiawar and Sanjan in Western India and settled there.

Gradually, they spread in small colonies, retaining their religious identity but adopting local customs. Known as Parsees (people of Persia), they make up barely 0.02% of the Indian population. Originally they were farmers, weavers and toddy-palm planters, but today they are some of India's biggest industrialists.

The holy book of Zendavestha contains the founder's sayings, known as Gathas. It advocates the worship of Ahu, the moving force and source of life. The luminous sun and the radiant fire are Zoroastrian symbols. The Parsees worship fire in their temples and always have a lighted lamp in their homes.

Parsee moral values stem from the motto, "Good thoughts, good speech and good deeds lead to perfect wisdom." The ceremonies exclusive to Parsees are Navjoth, the initiation into Zoroastrian ways, and Pateti or Navroze, the Parsee New Year. A distinctive feature is the Parsee funeral ceremony, when after prayers the body is offered to vultures and other birds of prey on top of a high hill, the Tower of Silence. The bones are then lowered into wells for dissolution.

"Like the rain water that falls into rivers and joins the mighty ocean, all forms of gods and their worship lead to the same Ultimate Being."

— Bhagavad Gita

TANTRIKAS

India has been the home of much of Asia's magic, medicine, folk beliefs and cults. These can be attributed to the materialistic view of cult groups, known as Tantrikas. In earlier times, they questioned the supremacy of the *Vedas*, rejected the Hindu caste system and denied the possibility of life after death. Their desire for prosperity "here and now" brought fertility cults of the mother goddess into the Tantrik fold. With it came the secret art of worshiping the life-giving sexual principle.

With elaborate diagrams, chants, charms and hand gestures, the rituals of the Tantrikas attempted to "bring to life" objects of worship. They practiced yoga, a form of exercise that unites the body and mind, and looked upon the creation of the universe as the blissful union of heaven and earth, spirit and form, male and female principles.

Perched on top of a huge rock, a yogi meditates.

While much of their philosophy has been absorbed into Hindu thought, some of their dubious practices were rejected outright by the majority, especially virgin sex-worship, black magic performances and spells cast to create a hold over people. These cults often operate in utmost secrecy, headed by a leader (*guru* or *swami*), and they shun public scrutiny.

LANGUAGE AND LITERATURE

A WESTERN scholar once observed, "Every Indian district has its own language and customs." There are more than 400 districts in India! What he was probably referring to are the several dialects spoken in towns and districts. India's states have been formed not by geo-political divisions but on the basis of the dominant language spoken.

The Indian Constitution recognizes fifteen state languages. Hindi and English are India's official languages. The Indian education system includes the study of three languages at school level: Hindi, English and the vernacular state language. This helps in developing multilingualism, while promoting the two official languages.

From prehistoric times until about the 11th century A.D., there were only two languages in India: Prakrit in the North and Tamil in the South. Pali, adopted by the early Buddhists, was an offshoot of Prakrit while Sanskrit served as the classical literary language of India, much as Latin did in the west. The development of spoken dialects into languages, each with its own distinct script and literature, is a phenomenon of the medieval period when religious devotees composed poems in dialect. It led to the growth of several languages.

Today, the two most widely used language groups are the Indo-Aryan and the Dravidian groups. Sanskrit belongs to the Indo-Aryan group. The ideas conveyed in texts of different languages, however, were commonly drawn from Sanskrit, which is considered the mother of most Indian languages. Thus, though Indian languages may appear to be varied, they do reflect a common culture.

Hindi and its variants are spoken by more than 40% of the population and are understood by more than 75% of Indians.

Opposite: **Indian calligraphy, a fine art form, carved on a wall.**

SCRIPTS

Indian scripts also have a common source. The earliest script, used until the 6th century A.D., for both Tamil and Sanskrit, was Brahmi.

Writing was not, however, the mode of transmitting knowledge in ancient India. Sitting close to the *guru* (teacher), the pupil learned verses orally through recitation. Yet, as early as the 4th century B.C., India had not only a well developed script but also the greatest of all known grammarians, Panini.

Today, all fifteen recognized state languages have their own scripts, derived mainly from the Indo-Aryan Sanskrit and the Dravidian Tamil. They are Assamese, Bengali, Gujarati, Hindi, Kannada, Kashmiri, Malayalam, Marathi, Oriya, Punjabi, Sanskrit, Sindhi, Tamil, Telugu and Urdu. Urdu, a product of Indo-Moslem fusion, is generally used by the Moslem community.

English education, introduced in the 19th century, has become a link-language for Indians throughout the subcontinent. It is also an important factor in the process of modernization, though its use is limited to cities and towns.

Rooftop classroom in a Rajasthan fort.

Palm leaves and tree bark once served as writing material and an iron stylus served as a pen. The stylus inscribed the letters on the leaves which were smeared with ink to darken the inscription, then excess ink on the leaf surface was wiped away. The bark and leaves were strung together upon a cord, so that all holy texts came to be called *sutras* or cords.

TAMIL TRADITION

The only writings that predate the influence of classical Sanskrit are in Tamil. Tamil literature seems to have begun with anthologies of secular lyrics known as *Sangam* poetry. Believed to be literary masterpieces of pre-Christian times, they contain some 1600 *sutras* or verses. Unlike *Sangam* poetry (and, incidentally, modern Tamil literature), most traditional Tamil literature is religious in form and content.

In the very early Christian era, a sage named Tiru Valluvar (1st or 2nd century A.D.), possibly a Jain monk, wrote beautifully precise moral aphorisms and two-line codes of ethics that are still taught to children. The 4th to the 9th centuries A.D. saw the growth of intensely rich devotional Tamil poems, forerunners to medieval Indian literature. They were songs in praise of the legendary gods, Shiva, Vishnu and Krishna. Poet-saints who wrote them were called Alwars and Nayanmars.

Children learning the alphabet in a village classroom.

Two romantic tales—*Silappadigaram* (Jain) and *Manimekhalai* (Buddhist)—were also composed between the 2nd and 5th centuries A.D. The Tamil version of the epic, *Ramayana*, was composed with great eloquence by Kamban, a 10th century poet.

Tamil literature thereafter went into a period of deep hibernation, perhaps because of political changes and a general weariness. Among modern poets, *Arunachala Kavi* and *Subramanya Bharatiyar* stand out for their simple and narrative forms of poetry.

SOUTHERN LANGUAGES

Tamil inspired the growth of regional languages in South India, such as Telugu in Andhra Pradesh, Kannada in Mysore and Malayalam in Kerala. These languages were also influenced by Sanskrit, the court language of many a South Indian ruler between the 8th and the 15th centuries.

The greatest Telugu poetry was produced during the time of the Vijayanagara Empire in the 16th century. The king, Krishna Deva Raya, was himself a renowned poet. But Telugu became the language of the South only after Saint Thyagaraja sang emotionally charged lyrical verses in classical melodies called *raga*.

An artist's rendition of "Geetha Govindam" where Krishna dances with the *gopis* (cowherd maidens).

Kannada also produced devotional poetry, the greatest of which was the 10,000-verse ballad, *Bharatesha Vaibhava*, written by the 16th century poet, Ratnakarvarni Varni. A dialect that has adopted the Kannada script is Tulu, widely spoken in the Malabar region.

Malayalam seems to have existed even earlier than the 9th century. Some of the literature produced in Malayalam suggests strong Buddhist influence. Apart from mystical verses or *Champus*, Malayalam developed a variety of dramatic literature suited for dance dramas, or *Kathakali*.

SANSKRIT LITERATURE

The earliest Sanskrit literature, the *Vedas*, probably dates back to 1500 B.C. Since the hymns had been passed down orally for several centuries before they were actually written down, nobody knows their exact origin. The *Rigveda* is the earliest text and consists of 1,028 hymns in praise of the gods of nature. The *Samaveda* is composed as musical *mantras* (chants), the *Yajurveda* is a book of mystical formulae, and the *Atharvaveda* contains magic and charms as medical prescriptions. Considered divine revelation, these four *Vedas* became the repository of all knowledge in the Indian subcontinent.

As Vedic philosophy was difficult to understand, *Old World Legends* known as *Puranas* were born. These imaginative tales about gods and goddesses helped the common man to understand ethical values.

Sanskrit dominated the literary scene for well over a thousand years. It inspired the growth of several languages and scripts in India, Central and Southeast Asia, living up to its epithet, *Deva Bhasha*—language of gods!

NORTHERN LANGUAGES

Although Prakrit is recognized as the forerunner to the North Indian languages, it would not be easy for someone who knows one of these languages to understand another without adequate exposure. Every language has produced its own literary masterpieces, some of which have crossed linguistic divisions and become famous throughout India.

Rabindranath Tagore with a family member.

Greatest among the vernacular literati was the 20th century poet, dramatist and artist, Rabindranath Tagore of Bengal, who won the Nobel prize for his collection of poems, *Geetanjali*. He evokes a unique sense of reverence among Indians in general and the Bengalis in particular.

Sant Kabir

Goswami Tulsidas

HINDI

Hindi is a product of several dialects spoken in Central and Northern India. All of them are folk dialects that trace their roots to Prakrit. Pure Hindi uses a liberal dose of Sanskrit and many Urdu words. Indians regard Hindi as ideal for communication but readily switch to English when it comes to technical subjects.

Several Hindu and Sufi mystics contributed to the enrichment of Hindi in the medieval period. The most outstanding was the 15th century poet, Sant Kabir. His soul-stirring verses, containing a fusion of Hindu and Moslem beliefs, are a landmark in the growth of Hindi. The greatest Hindi poet to date, however, is the 16th century saint, Goswami Tulsidas, whose devotional epic, *Ram Charith Manas*, retold the *Ramayana* in the language of the masses, making it the common man's scripture.

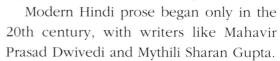

Modern Hindi prose began only in the 20th century, with writers like Mahavir Prasad Dwivedi and Mythili Sharan Gupta.

An offshoot of Hindi is Urdu, a word that means "military camp." It began as a campsite language of the Hindu and Moslem soldiers in the Hyderabad region of South India, and acquired Hindi vocabulary and Arabic script, thus blending language, thoughts and beliefs.

Bahadur Shah Zafar, the last of the Mughal emperors, Ghalib, and the 20th century poet, Mohammed Iqbal, are among the prolific Urdu poets, appreciated both in India and Pakistan.

GESTURES AND EXPRESSIONS

India's oral tradition has many gestures, expressions and proverbs. Greetings among friends invariably invoke a god's name. In the North, *Ram Ram* or *Jai Ramji Ki* (May Lord Rama live long and protect us) is a common greeting in the countryside, while *Vanakkam Swami* (I bow to You, O Divine One!) is a common welcome in the South. It is considered respectful to touch the feet of elders or prostrate oneself before them.

The expression for taking leave is "I'll go and come back" or "I'll be back," never simply "I'm going." Whatever the dialect, the latter means one is going out of this world forever!

It is common to address any man, known or otherwise, as "brother" and any woman as "sister." The correct form of address during speeches is also "Brothers and Sisters." Indians are generally articulate in their expressions and use facial and hand gestures liberally.

The most amazing uniformity exists in the oral tradition. Several proverbs such as "One who cannot dance blames the stage or finds fault with the floor," and "A dog's tail can never be straightened" are used in every Indian dialect.

In the last two hundred years, the influence of English on Indian language and literature has been significant. Prose literature and blank verse have invaded the literary world. To think in English and speak in the mother tongue, or vice versa, is now common among many.

Opposite bottom: **A Hindu devotee reading the** *Ramayana.*

Below: *"Namaskar."* **A woman touches the feet of an elder in greeting.**

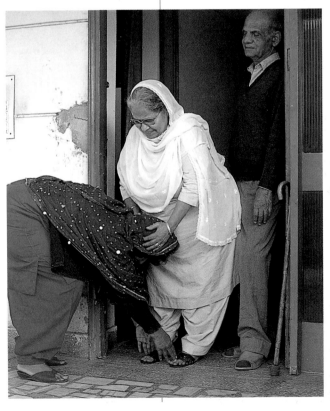

ARTS

NATURE AND PURPOSE

IN INDIA, art is not a pastime but a preoccupation, an expression of a way of life. It reflects India's philosophy, and its origins are as old as the history of the country. It has grown and developed at different levels to serve different functions. Whether it is jewelry beaten out of metal, delicate woven shawls and brocade *sari*, or carved ivory, wood and stone, few other nations have so exuberant a variety of arts.

The Indian performing arts do not have well-defined categories as in the west, such as opera, ballet, dance and drama. Very often it is an interesting blend of all these. Folk, ritual and classical forms exist side by side, influencing one another.

Yet, broad classifications are possible according to region, style and purpose. The folk arts, for instance, may be connected with social revelry after hunting, fishing or harvesting. The ritual or ceremonial arts are a mystical sort, performed as fertility temple rites. The classical arts are highly stylized and refined, and require years of training and academic scholarship.

Whatever the style or form, Indian arts convey a single theme: *rasa*, the essence of the joy of life. All Indian arts fuse with religious devotion, and this applies equally to music, dance, drama, poetry, painting, sculpture or handicrafts.

Opposite: **Paintings on the mud wall of a village hut. Art has no boundaries in India.**

Below: **The firm and deft strokes required for hand-painting takes a great deal of practice.**

SOME FOLK ART FORMS

In the Indian village, whether it is a festival celebrating spring or the monsoon season, the birthday of a mythic god or installation of a deity, houses and streets are decorated with folk motifs symbolizing prosperity and abundance. Cows, elephants and camels are also decked up for the occasion. Men, women and children sing, dance and enact tales of gods and goddesses all night long.

Each region has its own distinct style and form. The Punjab is famous for its rugged *Bhangra*, while Gujarat is known for its gentler *Garba* and *Raas* dances. The South Indian street dances are called *Therukkuthu*, while *Kavadi* and *Karagam* are more ritualistic dances, performed by devotees as wish-fulfilling prayers.

Community dances may contain magic, sorcery or religious ritual; such are the Lama dances of the Himalayan region, the *Chou* dance of East India and the *Theyiattam* of Kerala. Here, drama is added to rhythm and movement for fuller expression. With powerful percussion instruments, awesome characters recreate myths to depict the victory of good over evil.

POETRY IN MUSIC AND MOTION

All classical Indian art forms can be traced back to a single source—poetry. The recitation of the ancient *Vedas* is believed to have given rise to musical notes and scales. To this day it is poetry that is rendered as classical music. Dance, too, captures the poet's innermost feelings through mime and hand gestures. Dance is referred to as visual poetry, sculpture as frozen poetry.

In fact, all ancient works—whether fables or epic tales, science, mathematics or philosophy—were composed in poetic form. Verses were easier to memorize and hand down orally in the past, before paper and parchment came into use. Prose literature is a comparatively recent phenomenon.

Apart from abundant religious literature, Kalidasa's *Shakuntalam* in Sanskrit and Ilango Adigal's *Silappadigaram* in Tamil are among the famous secular works in ancient India. Subsequent contact with Islamic culture brought a fusion of Indian and Moslem thought. This is reflected in the *thumris* and *ghazals* (love poetry)

Raas dance.

In the agricultural cycle throughout Asia, the sowing time of March/April is full of festive celebrations. A 27-day festival in Orissa known as Chaitra Parva begins with fasting, bathing in holy water and praying. The devotees walk on fire and thorns and perform *Chou* masked dances, often falling into a trance. Then they pray to the fertility god Shiva and his consort Shakti, represented by a decorated pole and a water-filled pot.

MUSIC

Classical Indian music is spiritual in character. Sound is believed to have originated as a divine gift of the Lord of all Creation, Brahma. From this mystical origin, classical Indian music developed into a complex system as early as the 2nd century A.D. Temples served as places of learning and performing. Gods and goddesses provided the theme.

When Moslem rulers introduced music in their courts, romantic and secular music began to evolve with Persian and Central Asian elements. This gave rise to two distinct styles of music: the North Indian (Hindustani) and the South Indian (Karnatak).

Both styles are based on the system of *raga*, which means color or mood. A *raga* is a melodic base with characteristic ascending and descending notes. It conveys a mood or an emotion. In fact, there is a *raga* for every occasion—even for every part of a day! The individual interprets a melody to produce hours of improvised music. This is what makes Indian music different.

Indian music follows a rhythm cycle known as *tala*. Complex rhythmic patterns are woven in, and improvisation is allowed here as well. In a classical music ensemble, a violin or a *sarangi* (another string instrument played with a bow), and a percussion instrument (to mark the "beat") provide the accompaniment.

Shehnai, a wind-pipe instrument, and drums.

There are no notations in Indian music. The *guru* teaches his students by oral demonstration and much is learned through skillful listening and years of practice. Traditionally, the student lives with his *guru* and absorbs the master's technique.

MUSICAL INSTRUMENTS

There are about 500 different kinds of Indian musical instruments, each with a distinct shape and tone. Many are indigenous, some are of foreign origin, while a few are ingenious adaptations. Most can be divided into string, wind and percussion categories.

The most ancient of them all are the Indian drums and gongs. The term for the South Indian percussion, *mridangam* (body of clay), suggests its primitive beginnings. The highly refined modern *mridangam* is capable of producing a wide variety of sound effects. In the North, the *tabla*, a two-piece drum, possibly derived from the Arabic *tabl*, constitutes a vital part of Indian music today.

String instruments are of the bowing, plucking and striking kind. The simplest of all is the one-string "drone" (*ektara*) which the singing bards carry. The *veena*, popular in the South today, was prevalent even in Ashoka's time (2nd century B.C.).

The *sitar*, made popular by the famous classical music genius, Ravi Shankar, is derived from the Persian *sehtar* and adapted by the 13th century court poet, Amir Khusro. The *sarod* is evolved from Afghanistan's *rebab* while the western violin has found a permanent place among classical Indian instruments.

Wind instruments include the bamboo flute, and the reed-piped *nadaswaram* and *shehnai*. None of them has metallic keys as in their western counterparts. Clever manipulation of the finger-holes or stops is required.

Sarangi, a bowing instrument, and a drum.

North Indian *Kathak* dancers performing a modern ballet.

CLASSICAL DANCE

Classical dance in India is based on standards laid down by the sage Bharatha more than two thousand years ago. They pertain to footwork, hand gestures, facial expressions, dress and make-up. Five regional styles have evolved based on these forms.

The South Indian *Bharathanatyam* is one of the most popular forms. With elaborate costume, jewelry and hair-do, the dancer builds up intricate footwork in a half-seated posture. Hand gestures and facial expressions narrate mythic, heroic or romantic tales. One dancer enacts all the roles, switching from emotion to emotion—joy to anger, mirth, fear, anguish, sorrow and so on.

Kathakali is the mimetic or mime-like dance drama of Kerala. With huge headdress and heavily painted faces, men enact supernatural roles, often both male and female. Powerful percussion instruments accompany this outdoor dance, which is usually performed in the temple courtyard.

Odissi, the dance form of East India, is flowing and sensuous, reminding one of the beautiful sculptures of the Konarak temple in Orissa. *Manipuri* is another East Indian dance, the subtle movements of which resemble Burmese, Thai and Cambodian dances.

Kathak is the North Indian form which emphasizes footwork and swift, swirling pirouettes. Having entered the royal courts of the Moslem kings in the medieval period, *Kathak* has assimilated other cultural influences.

Kuchipudi and *Mohiniattam* are neo-classical dances of South India with strong folk elements in their music and in certain gestures.

Above: *Kathakali*, the mimetic dance-drama of Kerala.

Left: A famous *Bharatha-natyam* dancer.

THEATER

Traditional Indian theater is more like a dance drama; it is very different from the dialogue-based western drama. Rural regions have a whole array of folk forms such as musical opera, masked theater and puppetry. Generally, in Indian theater, a narrator links up plots and sub-plots and a clown provides humor in between. The rest of the cast is broadly classified into good or bad characters.

With a simple orchestra, a temporarily constructed wooden stage, and elaborate dress and make-up, actors and actresses entertain the villagers from dusk to dawn on festive occasions. Regional styles may vary, but the themes are generally from *Old World Legends*: the *Puranas*, the *Ramayana* and the *Mahabharata*.

Colorful cast of Indian puppets. These are operated by strings.

In the past, a whole social class of performers grew out of the theatrical tradition. Chakyars or Bhagavatars in the South, originally of the Brahmin caste, took to entertaining to teach the people moral values. The art of storytelling was taken up by Bhanas, the singing minstrels. Only temple dancers, known as Devadasis, were considered socially inferior.

Modern Indian plays are quite like plays performed on a western stage; mythical themes are replaced by social themes and dialogue dominates the show. Bombay and Bengal produce plays that are a blend of western and Indian theater.

Unfortunately, the cinema and television are fast replacing the stage in many rural and urban places. But the *Ramayana* and the *Mahabharata* have made a dramatic comeback in the form of television serials—old themes in a new medium.

ARCHITECTURE

India is full of artistic legacies from the past. One of the most obvious is Indian architecture, which is a tapestry of buildings in many art forms. Some are in total ruin, while others are astonishingly intact. The South Indian Hindu temples, for instance, are architectural masterpieces, and the Hoysala temple at Halebid in Mysore has been described as a "stone lace-work of moving magnificence."

At Elura in Hyderabad, craftsmen excavated huge mountain rocks, carved the walls into powerful pillars and statues, chiseled out the interior to fill it with amazing frescos, and finally carved a series of chapels and monasteries deep into the rock. Known as the Kailasa temple, the mountain abode of Lord Shiva, it is a stupendous architectural achievement.

Jain saint decorates a niche in Gwalior, Madhya Pradesh. Some of the finest sculptures are to be found in such niches carved out of cliff walls.

95

In the North, many temples were razed to make way for mosques, minarets and tombs in the medieval period. The 250-foot Qutb Minar, the Jama Masjid or Pearl Mosque and the tombs scattered all over the old city of Delhi testify to this transformation. Elsewhere, slender minarets and spired domes with intricate inlay work are reminders of Indo-Moslem art.

The British gave India the imposing Gateway of India in Bombay and the Victorian style palace of the Viceroy in New Delhi. Today, the latter is known as the Rashtrapathi Bhavan, the residence of the President of India. Some of the universities, churches and libraries in Bombay, Madras and Calcutta were built during India's colonial era.

Pondicherry is distinctly French in its structure, while Goa, near Bombay, shows a strong Portuguese influence.

LEISURE

LIFE MOVES at a slower pace in India than in many other countries, leaving plenty of time for leisure activities. The countryside revels in traditional pastimes such as street shows, indoor games such as chess, Indian ludo and five stones, outdoor games and competitive ones such as *kabaddi* (a team game of skillful breathing and dodging), racing and wrestling.

In the cities, most of the games introduced by the British are popular. Generally speaking, Bengalis prefer soccer, the Punjabis hockey and "Bombayites" cricket. In the mountainous regions, climbing, trekking and skiing are seasonal sports while in the coastal regions, swimming, fishing and boat-racing are the obvious choices.

In the realm of entertainment, India is known for its traditional storytellers—the bardic folk singers of the North or the Bhagavatars of the South—who weave tales with songs and mimicry, holding their listeners' attention for several hours. Some even double up as puppeteers to recreate myths and legends.

Opposite: **The kite-seller. The kites are simple, but the thick spools of string seem to attest to their capability.**

Above: **"Simon says, hands up!"**

STORYTELLING

The classical musician Bhagavatars sing their tales in temples, infusing them with religious and moral values. Of eternal interest, naturally, are the *Ramayana* and *Mahabharata*, which highlight the triumph of the righteous over the wicked.

Today, the movie theater has become the most popular form of entertainment and the television has invaded even the most remote villages. Movie heroes and heroines have cashed in on mass adulation and some have even taken on new roles in politics.

Above: **Passers-by offer prayers to a life-size Lord Krishna which adorns the truck.**

Right: **Hanuman flies a mountain of herbs to cure Lakshmana.**

Once there lived a king named Dasharatha who had three wives and four sons. His eldest son, Rama, was sent to the forest for fourteen years, just when he was about to be crowned, because the king was bound by the promises he had made to his youngest queen.

When Rama was in the forest with his wife, Sita, and brother, Lakshmana, a wicked and lustful king, Ravana, came in the guise of a sage and abducted Sita. Rama and Lakshmana, with the help of the monkey god, Hanuman, went in search of Sita. They killed Ravana and his mighty army and Rama returned to rule, his exile over.

In this tale, Rama stands for righteous duty, Sita for purity and truth, and Ravana for arrogant might and greed. The *Ramayana* is a living tradition in India and many other parts of Asia.

TRADITIONAL PASTIMES

Playthings in traditional societies tend to be few; much is left to ingenuity and imagination. Wooden or clay dolls that little children play with in India often resemble Hindu gods and goddesses because both toys and gods are made by the same craftsmen.

Girls either play with five stones, tossing them up in the air and catching them in a hundred different ways, or play jumprope or hopscotch. The swing is so popular throughout India that South Indians install permanent swings in their homes. North Indian women celebrate a festival called Teej when tall swings are set up amid groves of trees for the young and old to swing and sing in praise of the monsoon season.

Organized sporting events are usually a feature of festivals. In the colorful harvest festival of Onam in Kerala (August-September), beautifully decked boat processions culminate in exciting snakeboat races, very similar to the Chinese dragonboat races in Singapore and Hong Kong.

Bullock races and bull fighting are competitions that accompany the harvest festivals of Tamil Nadu, while camel races and polo take center stage in the desert festivals of Rajasthan. Then there are the coconut plucking contests, groundnut eating races, even bride winning feats in rural India. But top of the list here as elsewhere is when the traveling circus is in town, and folks from the villages come in busloads to see the show.

Indian girls playing "five stones" on a sidewalk.

GAMES FROM THE PAST

Indians are known to have spent long hours playing board games even in ancient times, and archeological digs have unearthed stone and ivory dice. Gambling and bull fighting are believed to have been introduced into South India by the Roman seafarers, while archery and hunting were the preserve of royalty even in Vedic times.

Chess is known to have originated in India and spread to West and Southeast Asia. The Malay tiger game has its origin in the Indian *puli kattu*, a board game played with three tigers to a dozen goats, represented by stones, shells or tamarind seeds.

The board game of *pacheesi* carved on the Elephanta walls (5th century A.D.) was so popular with King Akbar that he cut squares on the pavement of the palace quadrangle and played with pretty slave girls as living pieces. To this day, it is a common indoor game in villages.

Akbar introduced polo to North India (it apparently originated in Persia), from where it spread to England in the 19th century. Today, polo is played in Northwest India and the Himalayan regions.

Tiger and lion hunting, popular in the medieval period, especially among the maharajas, have now been replaced by "shooting" pictures of wildlife with a camera, thanks to the timely policy of wildlife protection.

KABADDI AND THE ART OF YOGA

Two outdoor games that are distinctly Indian and require considerable skill are *kabaddi* and *kho-kho*. Known as *hu-tu-tu* in Maharashtra and *chudi-kodu* in the South, *kabaddi* requires neither elaborate equipment nor sports arena. This simple game of breath control is played by two teams of men. Any number can play.

A space is divided by a line scratched on the ground and the teams gather on either side of the line. One player from team A runs into the court of team B, shouting "*kabaddi*" or "*hu-tu-tu,*" touches a member and quickly crosses over to his court before his breath runs out. The opponents in team B first try dodging him. When touched, they join together to prevent him from returning to his court till his breath runs out. If he succeeds in leaving the opponents' court before running out of breath, his team scores a point; if not, the other team scores.

The game is hysterical fun. Crowds cheer and jeer, and some bet heavily on the outcome as the game picks up momentum.

Kho-kho is an all-girl catching game involving two teams. It, too, has become one of India's national games.

Training the body and mind control are the objects of yoga and the martial arts of Kerala such as *kalari payat.* Some schools have begun teaching yoga to help children build supple bodies and a sharp intellect. The health conscious take morning walks and practice yoga in the gardens dotting Indian cities.

Opposite top: **Puli kattu.** Three tigers represented by shells and twelve goats represented by stones are moved around a roughly drawn surface. To score, the goats must completely encircle each tiger.

Opposite bottom: **Hunting, a sport for some Indians, is serious work for others. Constant practice is required.**

Below: **Children are encouraged to join yoga classes to discipline mind and body. Stretching exercises in the park are less taxing for this group of senior citizens.**

103

Ski resorts are holiday destinations of the rich and fashionable.

MODERN SPORTS

India has made some progress in the world of sports recently. Games are promoted, good facilities provided for sportsmen and sportswomen, and grants are awarded to the skilled and talented.

Soccer, hockey, basketball, volleyball and cricket are popular group sports played by many in urban India. Elite clubs and associations offer tennis, badminton, squash, golf and billiards, while skiing, skating, vintage car rallies and yachting are becoming popular with the more affluent.

The one game closest to most Indian hearts is cricket. When India's national team plays test matches, every ear is glued to the transistor radio providing the running commentary. When the Indian team won a test match a few years ago, Madras declared a holiday and revelers took to the streets, singing, dancing and setting off firecrackers.

India is the pioneer of the Asian Games, held for the first time in New Delhi in March 1951. When the 11th Asian Games returned to India in 1982, more than 30 countries were represented by about 5,000 participants in the spectacular event.

Above: **Residents of an Indian suburb share a pleasant hour or so. Sports are for the spectators as much as for the players.**

Left: **Hockey is a sport in which many Indians excel.**

FESTIVALS AND FAIRS

FESTIVALS are a colorful expression of Indian traditions: of harvesting patterns and changing seasons, of myths and legends, of social and spiritual renewal.

Indian festivals are bewilderingly diverse. Most of them have a religious character, some being an interesting fusion of Hindu-Buddhist, Hindu-Moslem or Hindu-Christian beliefs. Some are national, secular events, such as Republic Day or Independence Day. Many are confined to certain regions. A few are celebrated only by certain castes, clans or tribes.

With more than six religions celebrating the birth of their gods or saints, Indians have many occasions to rejoice. In fact, there is some social revelry or temple festivity every other day of the year. Hindu festivals are set by the Indian calendar which follows the lunar cycle. They also correspond to the agricultural cycle of sowing and harvesting.

In villages, a festival is invariably accompanied by a fair

Opposite: **Giant effigies are erected for the festival of Dussehra.**

Below: **Butterfly dancers in a street parade.**

or cultural performance. Celebrations may last a week or ten days. Hindu festivals often begin with fasting and end with feasting, making self-imposed discipline a prelude to joyous abandon. Plants, birds, animals—all have a part. At least on one occasion, even the spirits of the dead are invited.

Buddhist monks don ceremonial headdress for a Ladakhi festival.

COMMON FESTIVALS

All over India, the New Year is celebrated sometime in the Indian calendar month of Chaitra (mid-March to mid-April). It is called Gudi Padwa in Maharashtra, Nav Warih in Kashmir, and Varuda Pirappu in Tamil Nadu. The method and time of celebration change from place to place. Usually, singing and dancing culminate in a visit to a temple.

The second lunar month (April-May), known as Vaisaka, Baisakhi or Vesak, is auspicious for Hindus, Buddhists and Sikhs alike. The full moon day of Vaisaka is associated with the Buddha's birth, enlightenment and *nirvana* (release from the cycle of births and deaths). Interestingly, the Hindus regard it as the birth star of Shiva's son, Kartikeyan, who also grants "enlightenment" to his worshipers on this day!

Buddhists form a procession led by an image of the Buddha riding a chariot drawn by four horses. They go around the temple, prostrating themselves and chanting, offer prayers and light several candles at the altar, release caged birds and animals and perform acts of charity.

The first new moon day of April-May is the birth anniversary of Guru Hargobind who founded the Sikh movement called the Khalsa. The Sikh New Year, known as Baisakhi, is primarily a social occasion when the traditional *Bhangra* is danced all through the night. Villagers in Punjab dress colorfully, take out processions, drink, and sing in joyful abandon.

FESTIVALS OF FAMILY TIES

Although there is no Father's Day, Mother's Day or Senior Citizen's Day in India, there are many festivals to enhance family relationships.

In the North, during the festival of Raksha Bandhan, a girl ties a decorated silk thread around her brother's wrist and applies a red dot of vermilion powder on his forehead. She makes sweets for him as a symbol of her affection. Her brother in turn gives her gifts and promises to protect her all his life, thus strengthening the sibling bond.

The Karva Chauth (North) or Karadaya Nonbu (South) is a festival to bind the faith and affection between married couples. The woman prays for her husband's well-being and fasts for a day, at the end of which she is blessed with a happy married life.

A girl decorates her little brother during the festival of Raksha Bandhan.

Pitrupaksh or Shraddha is a ceremony devoted to ancestors. Sometime in the first fortnight of September, food and various prayers are offered to crows, who represent the spirits of the dead. Some Indians observe the ceremony on the death anniversary of relatives. The spirits are believed to descend upon earth to participate in the ceremony.

At around the same time, Moslems celebrate Shab-i-Barat, a day when God is believed to register man's actions and dispense his fate accordingly. It is an occasion for prayer, fasting and acts of charity, visits to family graves and offerings of flowers—all of which is followed by feasting and merrymaking.

FESTIVAL MYTHS AND LEGENDS

Every Hindu festival is associated with a mythological tale. In September-October, the important nine-day festival of Navarathri, followed by the Dussehra on the tenth day, is one such festival.

In Bengal, where the festival is called Durga Puja, huge images of the deity are installed in public places. On the tenth day, they are taken on a procession and immersed in rivers or lakes. In Gujarat, women sing and dance the traditional *Garba* and *Raas* around the deity. In Uttar Pradesh and Delhi, however, the story of *Ramayana* is recreated through street performances. On the tenth day, giant effigies of the ten-headed king, Ravana, and his brothers are burned, symbolizing the victory of righteousness.

In the South, the same festival is known as the Doll's Festival. Women arrange images of deities and dolls on a platform in their homes, invite lady friends over and give them coconuts, betel leaves, turmeric and vermilion powder as symbols of femininity and prosperity.

Above right: **Durga Puja. A group carries an image to the river for immersion.**

Below: **Figurines of Durga being sold in Calcutta.**

CALENDAR OF INDIAN FESTIVALS

Pongal	Jan	South	Harvest thanksgiving
Basant Panchami	Jan/Feb	North	Spring festival
Republic Day	Jan 26	Delhi, capitals	National holiday
Shivaratri	Feb/Mar	Pan-India	Lord Shiva festival
Desert Festival	Jan/Feb	Rajasthan	Jaisalmer (fort) festival
Khajuraho	Feb/Mar	Madhya Pradesh	Dance festival
Holi	Mar	North	Spring/Color festival
Gangaur	Mar/Apr	Rajasthan	Women's festival
Mahavir Jayanti	Mar/Apr	Pan-India	Jain festival
Easter	Mar/Apr	Pan-India	Christian festival
Jamshed Navroz	Mar	Maharashtra,	Parsi New Year
Varuda Pirappu	Apr	South	Tamil New Year
Vaisaka	Apr/May	Pan-India	Buddhist festival
Baisakhi	Apr/May	North	Sikh New Year
Meenakshi	Apr	Tamil Nadu	Goddess Meenakshi's marriage anniversary
Pooram	Apr/May	Kerala	Hindu temple festival
Id-ul-Fitr	May	Pan-India	Moslem festival
Hemis Festival	Jun/Jul	Ladakh, Jammu, Kashmir	Buddhist festival
Rath Yatra	Jul	Orissa	Hindu temple festival
Naag Panchami	Jul/Aug	Pan-India	Snake festival
Raksha Bandhan	Jul/Aug	North	Sibling festival
Amarnath	Jul/Aug	Kashmir	Lord Shiva festival
Teej	Jul/Aug	Rajasthan	Swing festival
Independence Day	Aug 15	Pan-India	National holiday
Onam	Aug/Sep	Kerala	Boat festival
Janmashtami	Aug/Sep	Pan-India	Lord Krishna's birthday
Id-ul-Zuha	Aug/Sep	Pan-India	Moslem festival
Ganesh Chathurthi	Aug/Sep	Pan-India	Ganesha festival
Dussehra	Sep/Oct/	Pan-India	Durga/Rama festival
Divali	Nov	Pan-India	Rama/Krishna festival
Guru Parb	Oct/Nov	North	Guru Nanak's birthday
Muharram	October	Pan-India	Moslem festival
Christmas	Dec 25	Pan-India	Christian festival

Legend has it that Mahishasura, a demon king with the head of a buffalo, became insolent with power and caused great pain to the pious and innocent. Angered by his arrogance, the combined energy of the Hindu Trinity—Brahma, Vishnu and Shiva—created Durga, a deity with a thousand arms. Mounted on a tiger or lion and armed with Shiva's trident, Vishnu's discus and Brahma's thunderbolt, she vanquished the demon. The legend symbolizes the triumph of intellect over ignorance, of inner force over brute strength.

FESTIVAL OF LIGHTS AND SPRING FESTIVAL

Divali or Deepavali ("rows of lights") in October-November is India's most popular festival. It is believed that Lord Krishna killed the demon king, Narakasura, on this dark night. According to another belief, Divali celebrates Lord Rama's return to rule after a 14-year exile. Yet another tradition has it that Lakshmi, goddess of wealth and prosperity, blesses the homes and offices of her devotees on this auspicious day. Whatever the legend, it is a day when the whole of India rejoices with almost unrestrained abandon.

Homes, shops and buildings are spring-cleaned and beautifully decorated with rows of lamps and candles. Several days prior to that, people start making sweet dishes and buying new clothes and jewelry for the occasion. Fireworks are the main attraction for children and adults alike. The young seek the blessings of the elders; many visit a temple.

The Spring Festival of the North, popularly known as Holi, is also replete with color, fun and gaiety. According to legend, Holika, the wicked aunt of a divine child, Prahlada, wished to burn the boy for uttering the name of God. Amazingly enough, the fire protected the child and burned his cruel aunt instead!

Huge bonfires are lit on the eve of Holi to mark the end of evil. Since Holi is also the water sport played by Lord Krishna and his cowherd maidens, people throw colored water and powder at each other, visit friends, eat, drink and dance in joy.

BIRTHDAYS OF GODS AND SAINTS

India celebrates the birthdays of several gods, saints, *gurus* (teachers) and prophets with great pomp. In villages, even local heroes receive the honor reserved for gods.

Rama's birthday is a grand affair in temples dedicated to him, but it takes on a special significance in Ayodhya, his birthplace. Krishna's birthday is even more colorful, with vignettes from Krishna's life unfolding at home, in temples and cultural centers. Young children dress up as little Krishna and indulge in the naughty acts described in legendary tales of his childhood.

Christians celebrate the birth of Jesus on Christmas Eve and Christmas Day, with scenes from the nativity enacted at home and in churches. Midnight service and Christmas morning mass are packed with people. The Christmas tree, Santa Claus, gifts and Christmas parties have all become favorite features, adopted even by many non-Christians in the cities.

Moslems congregate at mosques to celebrate Prophet Mohammed's birthday, Id-i-Milad. Falling in the third month of the Islamic calendar, this day is marked by special religious discourses and the distribution of alms to the poor.

Sikhs celebrate Guru Parb in October or November to mark the birthday of their founder, Guru Nanak. Jains flock to the ancient Jain shrine at Girnar in Gujarat on Mahavira's birthday, while Parsees celebrate Khordad Saal, Prophet Zoroaster's birthday, in their temples.

Opposite top: **Lakshmi, goddess of wealth**

Opposite bottom: **Deepavali fireworks.**

Below: **Guru Nanak, the founder of Sikhism.**

VILLAGE FAIRS

Whatever the sect or religion, fairs are an integral part of festivity in India. They attract scores of residents from the neighboring villages, dressed in all their finery, on camels, in bullock carts, on bicycles and on foot. Hectic buying, bargaining and selling are the order of the day. Anything from kitchen utensils, trinkets and fresh vegetables, to cows and horses are bought and sold. It is also the ideal time for selecting brides and grooms! Magic shows, street dances, puppet theater, folk music, circus shows and impromptu acts add to the festive spirit of the fairs.

Elephant rides and camel races are common in Teej and Pushkar fairs in Rajasthan. Bull fighting is a regular feature on the day following the harvest festival (mid-January) of Pongal in the South. Cockfights involving heavy betting are also common then. Boat races are popular with the seafarers and fishermen of Kerala during the festival of Onam.

In mountainous Ladakh, the annual fair at the advent of spring includes a Buddhist ritual art in monasteries. The actors and musicians are Lamas or monks, blowing huge trumpets and clapping cymbals and drums. Masked figures, gorgeously attired in silk robes, represent spirits and demons. The victory of good and the defeat of the demons are enacted with stunning effect.

Jains hold an Arathyatra fair in Meerut in the North to celebrate the birth of three of their saints, called Tirthankaras. The full moon day in October-November sees more than a million Jains flocking to the fair.

Opposite: **Barefoot on live coals in a test of faith. Fire-walking is sometimes the fulfillment of a vow.**

Below: **Rides on elephants and ferris wheels are part of the fun in festival fairs.**

TESTS OF FAITH

Fire-walking is a common test of faith among many rural Indian communities. Once a year in the South, it serves as a wish fulfilling ritual performed either in honor of local deities or to ensure a good harvest. "Hero youths" bathe in the temple complex, smear their bodies with turmeric and walk on a bed of live coals.

Moslems, especially the Shias, commemorate the martyrdom of Imam Hussain, the grandson of Prophet Mohammed, with a month of fasting and prayers. Known as Muharram, it is a solemn period observed with great fervor in Lucknow, where bands of men walk on a bed of live coals, watched by thousands. Some even lash themselves with whips in a show of grief.

Goans celebrate a festival called Zatra to mark the visit of three eastern kings to Bethlehem, the birthplace of Jesus Christ. Three young men dressed as kings walk up to a church which shelters a sculpture of the Holy Infant. Their entrance kicks off feasting and dancing. Breathtaking fire-walking and fire-eating feats are also performed.

In January, pious devotees of the god Aiyappa abstain from meat, alcohol and sex, impose other forms of severe discipline on themselves and walk barefoot several miles up the hill of Sabari Malai in the South.

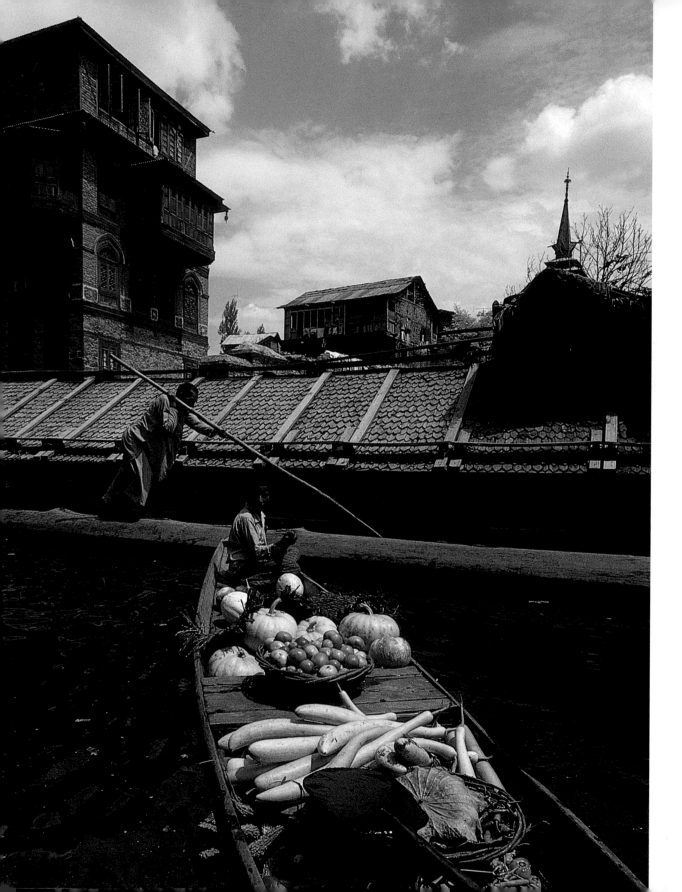

FOOD

"YOU ARE what you eat" is an old saying in India where food is considered as sacred as the human body. Indians look for a balanced nourishment of both body and mind in their daily diet in the belief that food influences behavior, attitudes and well-being.

Spices, milk and milk products, meat, lentils and vegetables are used in varying degrees, depending on the season, month or day they are consumed. All foods have been classified by an ancient science into heating and cooling agents. Indians know, for instance, that mangoes produce heat and milk or milk curd (yogurt) cools the body. So children are given a glass of milk after they eat mangoes to prevent boils and sores in the heat of summer—and it works!

Each food item is believed to have certain qualities that are transmitted to the consumer. Meat, alcohol and highly fermented foods are considered base foods that cause laziness and greed. Rich and oily foods, having excess spice or sugar, are considered royal foods that produce a quick temper and a love for luxury. The Indian who wishes to calm the body and sharpen the mind would live on a diet of milk products, fresh vegetables and fruits, lentils, nuts and cereals.

The man in the street is hardly aware of such food values, but they have influenced his daily diet and eating habits greatly.

Opposite: **Vegetable-seller bringing his goods to the market by boat.**

Left and below: **Stalls selling fruits like mangoes and bananas are nearly everywhere in India.**

FOOD VARIETIES

Indian food is as rich and varied as the country itself, for each region has its distinct specialities. A typical Indian meal consists of cereal, lentils (known as *dhal*), vegetable, meat or fish, and some yogurt.

Depending on the region, the cereal could be rice, or any of a variety of Indian wheat breads: *chapati, puri, naan* or *paratha*. A poor man's diet might well be just a glass of rice porridge or plain *roti* (Indian bread) with raw onions and green chilli. In many middle-class homes, both *chapati* and rice, often spiced and garnished with vegetables and nuts, are served.

Lentils form a major source of protein for Indians and India produces a large variety of split peas and beans. They are taken daily, and many spices have been used to create a whole range of differently flavored dishes.

Vegetables in season—including gourds, greens and root vegetables—are popular throughout India. Raw banana curries and pumpkin with a liberal dash of freshly grated coconut are typical in the South, while a dish of capsicum and cauliflower in onion, garlic and tomato gravy is popular in the North.

Fish and prawns are hot favorites in the coastal regions, while egg and chicken preparations are common throughout India. Islamic influence is seen in the variety of royal Mughal style recipes in thick gravies. Their conical earthen oven, called *tandoor*, has added a rich spread of oven-cooked *tandoori* breads (*naan*, for example) and *tandoori* meats like chicken and mutton to the Indian menu.

MILK AND CURD IN THE LAND OF KRISHNA

Milk and milk products form an essential part of the Indian diet, especially yogurt, which in India is known as *dahi* or *thairu*. Yogurt neutralizes the chilli heat of hot spices, cools the system in the heat of Indian summer and acts as an excellent digestive. It is prepared daily in many homes. Yogurt is taken plain, salted, or sweetened with sugar, as well as with spices and salad vegetables. Sour yogurt is cooked into sauces or added to stewed vegetables, while plain yogurt is thinned into a special cool drink called *lassi* or *moru*.

Street vendor cooling milk. It is drunk plain or laced with spice.

Ghee (clarified milk fat), once regularly used as a cooking base, is now added "just for the flavor," thanks to rising costs and health consciousness. On special occasions, however, candy is prepared only with ghee. Many indigenous medicines are mixed in ghee for the intrinsic qualities it is believed to possess. Ghee is offered to the spirits and gods in ritual ceremonies.

Yogurt and ghee are the favorite foods of Krishna, the cowherd god. On his birthday, homes and temples serve delicious candy and snacks made with milk and ghee. In the North, they make *rasagulla* (cottage-cheese balls soaked in syrup), *barfi* (diamond-shaped cakes), or mix sugar and cardamom with milk curd and churn it into *srikhund*.

South Indians stir milk, sugar and seasoning into a condensed sticky sweet called *thirati paal*, or add coconut and flour to make sweet balls called *laddu*. All this for their favorite god, Krishna!

INDIAN HERBS AND SPICES

Herbs and spices are a special feature of Indian cooking. They not only enhance flavor but act as stimulants, digestives, tonics and antiseptics. In fact, a whole system of ancient medicine, known as *ayurveda*, was developed from them.

Today, while many spices and herbs may be confined to Indian pharmacy shelves, many others have become a part of daily use, either as preventives or as simple home remedies. Asafoetida, a very pungent plant gum resin, is considered so beneficial for wind and acidity problems that a pinch of asafoetida powder is a must in Indian cooking, especially in the South. Some of the other spices regarded essential for cooking are pepper, fenugreek, clove, cinnamon, turmeric, dried ginger and coriander.

Commonly used leaves are the betel, basil, mint and curry leaves. Known as *paan*, betel is a creeper that grows profusely in most parts of India. Indians use them on auspicious occasions, as well as chew them with betelnut after meals to digest food and prevent stomach upsets. Some just love its juice which coats their mouth a deep red. Many chew *paan* with tobacco and grow addicted to it.

Basil or *tulasi*, grown in every home and temple garden, is both sacred and medicinal. It is ideal for coughs and asthma, and its leaves are offered to the gods then eaten as blessed food. Mint is considered a stimulant. Curry leaf, which is high in Vitamin C, has an exotic flavor.

Paan **stall. These small packages of spices wrapped in betel leaf are popped into the mouth and chewed with relish.**

121

HABITS AND PRACTICES

A thorough rinsing of hands, legs and face is common before a meal where people sit on the floor and eat with their fingers. Food is offered first to the gods and then served by the woman of the house, who eats after everyone else has finished.

Indians generally eat with their hands and use stainless steel or brass vessels and plates. While the rich use silver plates, many Indians in the South use rectangular sections of banana leaf for plates. In many urban homes, food is served on a western style dining table set out with cutlery. A glass of water is served first.

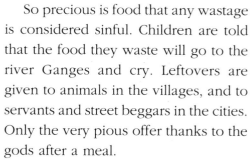

So precious is food that any wastage is considered sinful. Children are told that the food they waste will go to the river Ganges and cry. Leftovers are given to animals in the villages, and to servants and street beggars in the cities. Only the very pious offer thanks to the gods after a meal.

Eating times vary from region to region. South Indians do not eat breakfast generally, but have a very early brunch. Bengalis are known to have very late dinners, 10 or 11 o'clock at night being quite normal! Gujaratis eat their food at sunset and snack on fruit juice or dessert later in the night.

TABOOS AND PREFERENCES

Abstinence from food and drink is part and parcel of an Indian's life. This may take the form of a temporary fast, or avoidance of particular foods, or both. Most Indians avoid meat on occasion and many are vegetarian all their life. Beef to Hindus and pork to Moslems are forbidden foods. Moslems eat only *halal* meat and other foods, that is, meat or other products of animals slaughtered according to Islamic law.

Brahmins, some of the Hindu merchant communities, Jains and many Buddhists are strict lacto-vegetarians. They consume milk products but abstain from all other animal foods such as eggs, fish, chicken and meat. Orthodox Brahmins and Jains avoid onions, garlic, coffee and tea, as all these are believed to activate baser passions. Strict food habits and a disciplined diet are considered essential for a spiritual life.

Above: **The candy and crackers vendor.**

Opposite top: **A typical North Indian *thali* or stainless steel plate, containing a "set meal" of vegetables, *dhal*, curd, rice and *chappati*.**

Opposite bottom: **A wedding feast.**

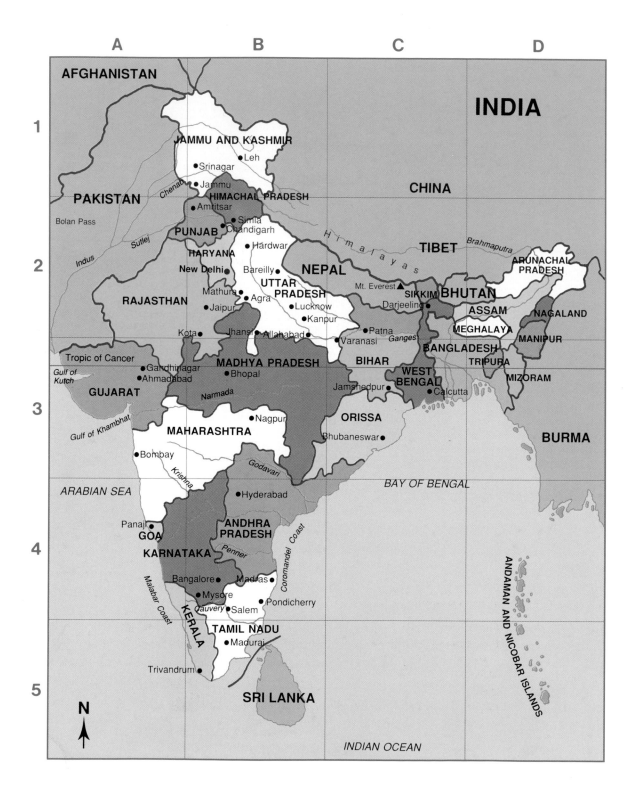

Afghanistan A1
Agra B2
Ahmadabad A3
Allahabad B2
Amritsar B2
Andaman Islands D4
Andhra Pradesh B4
Arabian Sea A4
Arunachal Pradesh D2
Assam D2

Bangalore B4
Bangladesh C3
Bareilly B2
Bay of Bengal C4
Bhopal B3
Bhubaneswar C3
Bhutan C2
Bihar C3
Bolan Pass A2
Bombay A3
Brahmaputra D2
Burma D3

Calcutta C3
Cauvery B4
Chandigarh B2

Chenab A1
China C1
Coromandel Coast B4

Darjeeling C2

Gandhinagar A3
Ganges C3
Goa A4
Godavari B3
Gujarat A3
Gulf of Khambhat A3
Gulf of Kutch A3

Hardwar B2
Haryana B2
Himachal Pradesh B2
Himalayas C2
Hyderabad B4

Indian Ocean C5
Indus A2

Jaipur B2
Jammu B1
Jamshedpur C3
Jhansi B2

Kanpur B2

Karnataka A4
Kashmir B1
Kerala B5
Kota B2
Krishna A4

Leh B1
Lucknow B2

Madhya Pradesh B3
Madras B4
Madurai B5
Maharashtra B3
Malabar Coast A4
Manipur D3
Mathura B2
Meghalaya D2
Mizoram D3
Mt. Everest C2
Mysore B4

Nagaland D2
Nagpur B3
Narmada B3
Nepal C2
New Delhi B2
Nicobar Islands D5

Orissa C3

Pakistan A2
Panaji A4
Patna C2
Penner B4
Pondicherry B4
Punjab B2

Rajasthan A2

Salem B4
Sikkim C2
Simla B2
Sri Lanka B5
Srinagar B1
Sutlej A2

Tamil Nadu B5
Tibet C2
Tripura D3
Trivandrum B5
Tropic of Cancer A3

Uttar Pradesh B2

Varanasi C3

West Bengal C3

International Boundary
State Boundary
Tropic of Cancer
▲ Mountain
● Capital
● City
River

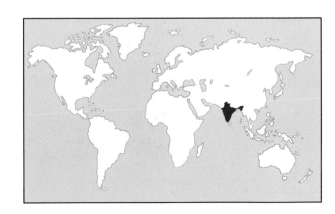

QUICK NOTES

LAND AREA
1.27 million square miles

POPULATION
835 million

CAPITAL
New Delhi

STATES
Andhra Pradesh, Arunachal Pradesh, Assam, Bihar, Goa, Gujarat, Haryana, Himachal Pradesh, Jammu, Karnataka, Kashmir, Kerala, Madhya Pradesh, Maharashtra, Manipur, Meghalaya, Mizoram, Nagaland, Orissa, Punjab, Rajasthan, Sikkim, Tamil Nadu, Tripura, Uttar Pradesh, West Bengal

NATIONAL SYMBOL
Ashokachakra, the wheel associated with King Ashoka, found on the Indian flag, the rupee coin and the Ashokan Pillar.

MAJOR RIVERS
Brahmaputra, Ganges and Indus

HIGHEST POINT
Kanchenjunga (28,208 feet)

CLIMATE
Six seasons: winter, spring, summer, summer monsoon, fall and winter monsoon

NATIONAL/OFFICIAL LANGUAGES
English and Hindi, in addition to these state languages: Assamese, Bengali, Gujarati, Hindi, Kannada, Kashmiri, Malayalam, Marathi, Oriya, Punjabi, Sanskrit, Sindhi, Tamil, Telugu and Urdu

MAJOR RELIGION
Hinduism

CURRENCY
Rupee
(US$1 = 17 rupees)

MAIN EXPORTS
Agricultural products, textiles, jute, chemicals, leather goods, iron and steel, precious stones

IMPORTANT ANNIVERSARIES
Republic Day (January 26); Independence Day (August 15)

LEADERS IN POLITICS
Mohandas Karamchand Gandhi—independence fighter who led peaceful protest marches
Pandit Jawaharlal Nehru—first Prime Minister of India
Indira Gandhi—longest serving Prime Minister of India

LEADERS IN LITERATURE
Nissim Ezekial (poet)
Girish Karnad (playwright)
Dom Moraes (poet)
R.K. Narayan (writer)
Vikram Seth (writer)
Rabindranath Tagore (poet)

GLOSSARY

Aryan	Indian race of mixed origin, believed to be Indo-European.
caste	Social class, originally based on occupation. Some of these are the Brahmins (priestly caste), Vaishyas (merchant caste) and Sudras (laboring caste)
Dravidian	Indigenous Indian race.
guru	Teacher.
Hanafi	One of four teachings of the Sunni sect.
Hindu Trinity	Brahma the creator, Vishnu the preserver and Shiva the destroyer.
subcontinent	Large self-contained land mass which forms a subdivision of a continent.
Sunni law	Islamic law based on the word of Prophet Mohammed, but not attributed to him.
Vedas	*Books of Knowledge,* sacred writings composed about 1500 B.C. These are mainly *Rigveda, Samaveda, Atharvaveda, Yajurveda, Brahmanas* and *Upanishads. Veda* means knowledge in Sanskrit.

BIBLIOGRAPHY

Galbraith, Catherine Atwater and Rama Mehta: *India, Now and Through Time,* Houghton Mifflin, Boston 1980.

Rai, Usha and Rai, Raghu (Photographer): *India,* Times Travel Library, Times Editions, Singapore 1990.

Sarin, Amita Vohra: *India—An Ancient Land, A New Nation,* Dillon Press, Minneapolis, 1985.

INDEX

Picture Credits

Neil Beer, Sheila Brown, Jon Burbank, Joginder Chawla, Jane Duff, G.A. Grinsted, Libby Howells, Indian High Commission of Singapore, Indian Tourist Bureau of Singapore, Ng Toon Juan, Raghu Rai, Veronique Sanson, Radhika Srinivasan, Straits Times, Diane Wilson

REFERENCE